past perfect

The Martha Hester Collection of Vintage Alexander Dolls

By Florence Theriault

Gold Horse Publishing

© Copyright 2009 Theriault's Gold Horse Publishing. All rights reserved.

No part of this book may be reproduced or utilized in any form or by any means, electronic or mechanical, including photocopying, recording, or by an information retrieval system, without permission, in writing, from the author or the publisher.

To order additional copies contact:
Dollmasters, PO Box 2319, Annapolis, MD 21404
Tel. 800-966-3655   Fax 410-571-9605
www.dollmasters.com

Design: Travis Hammond
Photography: Gerald Nelson

$49
ISBN: 1-931503-60-5
Printed in Hong Kong

This antique doll collection auctioned by Theriault's of Annapolis, Maryland, November 1, 2009.

www.theriaults.com.

In the quest for vintage Alexander dolls, one must often make a choice: the rare or the perfect. But not always. There are those times when serendipity happens. The rare and the perfect combine. Dolls appear as they left the shelves half a century ago. Tenderly-arranged coiffures, delicately blushed cheeks, costumes as crisp and fresh as ever they were. And then at a happy second glance, you notice that they are the rare, oh-so-rare models that appear on the market only a few times each decade. Such is the collection of the late Martha Hester of Houston, Texas, whose dolls were among those featured in the book Madame Alexander Dolls, An American Legend.

1. Complete Set of Cloth Little Women with Original Boxes

16" (41 cm.) The four all-cloth dolls have suede-like facial complexion with hand-painted facial features, side-glancing brown eyes, small bow-shaped lips, soft mohair wigs with delicate curls in various shades of brunette and blonde, stitch-jointed five piece bodies. Costumes: each is wearing her original tagged cotton gown, petticoat, pantalets, socks, shoes. Each costume is tagged with name of doll and Little Women, Madame Alexander Dolls (three are designated copyright, one is Trademark Pending), and each doll is presented in her original labeled box. Excellent unplayed with condition, costumes very fresh, nose tip rubs. Alexander, 1933-34, the dolls were presented by Madame Alexander to coincide with the RKO release of the Little Women film starring Katherine Hepburn. $2000/3000

2. Charming Cloth Little Shaver Baby

12" (30 cm.) The all-cloth baby has a mask pressed and printed face with hand-painted details especially of eyes, blonde yarn curly hair, and peach muslin body. Costume: pink organdy baby dress with matching bonnet edged with lace, slip, flannel diaper, knit booties. The costume is tagged Madame Alexander, New York, and the doll is preserved in her original box with pink paper label and has her original gold paper label. Near mint condition. Alexander, Little Shaver Baby, 1941. $400/600

3. Bridesmaid in Yellow Gown from 1940s Bridal Party Ensemble

20" (51 cm.) All composition, socket head, five piece composition body, brown sleep eyes, dark eye shadow, closed mouth, brunette mohair shoulder-length wig in soft curls. Costume: sheer nylon yellow gown over attached faille petticoat, the gown decorated with golden-yellow silk-like ribbons and streamers, yellow panties, shoes, matching yellow muff decorated with delicate pastel flowers, and a lovely bouquet of matching flowers in her hair. The costume is tagged Madame Alexander and the doll is preserved in original box. Near mint condition with beautiful patina of perfectly preserved complexion, original coiffure, fresh and bright original costume. Alexander, from the 1940 Bridal Party series. $700/1100

4. Godey Lady in Lilac Taffeta with Exquisite Floral Clusters, 1949

14" (36 cm.) All hard plastic with socket head and five-piece body, blue/green sleep eyes, platinum-blonde hair in centerpart with primly-arranged curls at each side of head. Costume: lilac taffeta faille gown with lace trim, wide embroidered cotton collar, silk-like sash, full-length petticoat, pantalets, socks and shoes. Her hair and sash are decorated with delicate lilac and blue floral clusters and she holds a matching corsage on her wrist. The gown is tagged Godey Lady, Madame Alexander, and she has a clover tag on her wrist labeled Godey Lady. She is preserved in her original box labeled Godey with Fashion Award seal. Near mint condition with lovely complexion and pristine crisp costume and accessories. Alexander, 1949. $800/1200

5. Red-Haired Nina Ballerina, 1951/52

21" (53 cm.) All hard plastic, swivel head with Margaret face, five piece body, blue sleep eyes, center-part red hair pulled away from face at each side and captured in a cluster of curls at her back crown with rolled curls at her nape. She is wearing an ivory satin tutu with ivory tulle skirt arranged with draped design and decorated with little flowers at each drape, satin panties, white stockings, magenta satin shoes, and having a paper Fashion Award. Her costume in tagged Nina Ballerina, Madame Alexander, and she is presented in her original labeled box. Near mint condition with very beautiful blush and complexion, rare hair color in original coiffure, fresh costume. Nina Ballerina, model #1849 from 1951/52. $700/900

6. Cinderella with Gilded Woven Coronet and "Glass" Slippers, 1950

14" (36 cm.) All hard plastic, socket head with Margaret face, five piece body, platinum hair in elaborate coiffure with braided coronet and pageboy curls at the nape, and blue sleep eyes. Costume: pale aqua satin gown with pouf sleeves and panniers, silver metallic edging and stars, matching petticoat, panties, and having stockings, "glass" slippers, necklace, bracelet and metallic coronet. The costume is tagged Madame Alexander, she has a gold paper clover tag on her wrist labeled Cinderella and she is in her original labeled box. Near mint condition with beautiful complexion, blush, coiffure, fresh costume. Alexander, 1950. $700/900

7. Walt Disney's Snow White with Exceptional Coiffure, 1950

14" (36 cm.) All hard plastic, socket head, five piece body, blue sleep eyes, ebony-black hair in perfect original coiffure with scalloped-edge waves around the forehead then forming into rolled curls at the nape held by a rose ribbon. Costume: gilt-flecked rose taffeta gown with gold metallic laced vest, petticoat, panties, socks, gold shoes. The costume is tagged Snow White, Madame Alexander. She has two original Snow White tags on her wrist including an unusual green tag, and is presented in her original labeled box. Near mint condition. Alexander, model 1535, 1950. $600/900

8. Peggy Bride with Beautiful Complexion and Coiffure, 1950
14" (36 cm.) All hard plastic, socket head, five piece body, strawberry-blonde mohair wig with soft curls captured under a scalloped-edge satin headband with floral trim and cascading veil, blue sleep eyes. Costume: chiffon ivory wedding gown with attached underslip and chemise, demure Peter Pan collar and tiny bead buttons, panties, stockings with single garter, ivory shoes, and carrying a wrist bouquet. The costume is tagged Madame Alexander New York and she wears her original paper clover leaf wrist tag, and is presented in her original box. Near mint condition with very beautiful satin-like complexion enhanced with delicate blush. Alexander, the Peggy Bride model was presented in 1950.
$700/900

9. Superb and Pristine Margaret Rose, c. 1949

18" (46 cm.) All hard plastic, socket head, five piece body, large sleep eyes, closed mouth, soft brunette curls with forehead bang. Costume: pale pink sheer nylon full-length gown with lace trim and collar, rose satin sash and bonnet streamers, wide-brimmed bonnet; bouquets of shaded rose buds at her waist and decorating the bonnet, attached silk-like petticoat, panties, ribbed knit stockings, black side-snap shoes with fabric bows. Her costume is tagged Margaret Rose, Madame Alexander, and she has a paper clover leaf tag also labeled Margaret Rose. The doll is preserved in her original box with Margaret Rose stamped on the base along with her original price of $10. Near mint condition with superb complexion, coiffure and costume. Alexander, Margaret Rose, c. 1949. $900/1200

10. "Everybody Loves a Bride" with Fashion Award, 1952

18" (46 cm.) All hard plastic, socket head, five piece body, dark blue sleep eyes, ruby lips, dark brunette hair with curled bangs and pageboy curls. She is wearing an ivory satin gown with superb torchon lace yoke and collar, the yoke trimmed with tiny rhinestones, petticoat, panties, white stockings, flat shoes. A lace-edged tulle coronet and veil is trimmed with a coronet of roses and leaves that match the bouquet she holds. The gown is tagged Madame Alexander, and she has a gold paper fashion award on her wrist. Near mint condition, very beautiful complexion, hair appears never removed from net, and costume is pristine. Alexander, the bride appeared as model #1850 in the 1952 catalog with blonde or brunette hair, available in three sizes, and described as "everybody loves a bride". $800/1200

11. Flocked Hair Groom with Brass Fashion Award from 1950 Bridal Group, 1950

18" (46 cm.) All hard plastic, socket head, five piece body, brown sleep eyes, brunette side-parted hair cropped closely to head and tightly smoothed. She is wearing a bridegroom ensemble comprising black pleated pants, short formal jacket with wide lapels and long tails, pique shirt with bow-tie and rhinestone pin, white pique cummerbund, boutonniere, black stockings and black shoes. His costume is tagged Madame Alexander New York, and he has an embossed brass Fashion Award bracelet, and he has his original box labeled Groom. Near mint condition, superb complexion and hair, very fresh and crisp costume. Alexander, Groom from the 1950 Bridal Group. $800/1000

12. Rosamund Bridesmaid in Rose Taffeta Gown, 1951
18" (46 cm.) All hard plastic with socket head, five piece body, blue sleep eyes, blonde hair with bangs, her hair waved back and captured at the sides of her face, with curls tumbling onto her shoulders. Costume: pale rose taffeta gown with tulle overskirt and sleevelets, rose taffeta panties, stockings, rose satin shoes. A woven green wide headband is decorated with clusters of pale pink rosebuds and there are two rosebuds at her waist. She has an embossed brass Fashion Award wrist tag and is preserved with her original box with Fashion Award seal. Her condition is pristine with outstanding complexion and fine blushing, perfect coiffure, crisp and fresh original costume. Alexander, Rosamund Bridesmaid, 1951-52. $900/1400

73. Rosamund Bridesmaid in Yellow Tulle Gown, 1953
18" (46 cm.) All hard plastic, five piece body, large blue sleep eyes, brunette curly hair,. She is wearing a yellow full-length gown of richly gathered tulle over nylon with gathered tulle straps that form into sleevelets, matching panties, stockings, satin shoes, and a matching yellow headband that is decorated at each side with a cluster of tiny yellow flowers and rose buds; there are two yellow rosebuds at her waist and tiny flowers sprinkled here and there on her skirt. The dress is tagged Madame Alexander New York. Near mint condition with beautifully blushed satiny complexion, ruby lips, perfect original coiffure, and crisp bright costume, with hat box. Alexander, Rosamund Bridesmaid, model #1851, 1953. $900/1400

14. Wendy Bride in Tulle and Taffeta Gown, 1953

18" (46 cm.) All hard plastic, socket head, five piece body, blue sleep eyes, blonde hair with original rolled curls still retaining their pins. Costume: wedding gown of tulle over white taffeta, having scooped neck, tulle pouf sleeves, panties, shoes, stockings, white cap with border trim of tiny florets that appear to simulate the lilies of the valley that decorate the cap. She is carrying a bouquet of flowers and a classic hat box. The costume is marked "Madame Alexander New York and she is presented in her original box stamped Wendy with fashion award symbol. Near mint condition, pristine coiffure, beautiful rosy complexion, crisp and fresh costume. Alexander, the Wendy Bride was presented in their 1954 catalog as model #1855. $900/1200

15. Flower Girl with Circlet of Flowers, 1954

18" (46 cm.) All hard plastic, socket head, five piece walking style body, sleep eyes, short ash blonde hair in curls and curly bangs. She is wearing a "fluffy nylon net and lace dream dress over taffeta", as described in the Alexander 1954 catalog, along with a sash of pink satin and "a circlet of flowers in her hair". The dress is tagged Madame Alexander, New York. Near mint condition, beautiful complexion, original hair pins never removed from hair, crisp and fresh costume, original hat box. Alexander, the doll appeared as model #1835 in the 1954 catalog named Flower Girl. $600/900

16. Very Rare Transitional Bride in Pristine Condition, 1955

18" (46 cm.) Hard plastic socket head, hard plastic torso and legs jointed at hips and knees, vinyl arms with shoulder and elbow jointing, blue sleep eyes, reddish/brown hair with original bangs and curls. She is wearing her original ivory satin brocade wedding gown with tulle ruffles at the shoulders, dart-shaped waist, widely-flared skirt and a border of ivory sequins at the neckline, with panties, stockings, and shoes, and a coronet of rose and white tiny flowers in her hair that form into an extended tulle veil and match the floral bouquet that she holds. The costume is tagged Madame Alexander New York, and the booklet on her wrist references the year 1955; the doll is a transitional model with earlier face and Binnie-style body introduced that year. Near mint condition, gorgeous complexion and hair, costume perfectly preserved including flowers. Alexander, 1955. $700/1100

17. Binnie Bridesmaid with Silver Slippers, 1955

18" (46 cm.) Hard plastic socket head, hard plastic torso and legs that are jointed at hips and knees, vinyl arms jointed at shoulders and elbows, blue/green sleep eyes, brunette curly hair with bangs. Costume: pink tulle gown over pink nylon with ruffled collar and sleeves, flounced silk-like sash, unusual hip-length hoop, panties, stockings, silver slippers. She has a generous circlet of shaded flowers in her hair that matches the flowers sprinkled on her skirt, and she wears a "diamond" ring. The costume is tagged Binnie Walker, and she is preserved with her original box labeled 1846. Madame Alexander. Near mint, gorgeous facial complexion and blush, perfect coiffure and fresh, crisp costume. Alexander, model #1846, 1955 $800/1200

19. Binnie Walker with Faux-Leopard Accessories and Red Hat Box, 1954

15" (38 cm.) All hard plastic, socket head, five piece walking style body, blue/green eyes, blonde hair in stylist original coiffure. Costume: tattersall-plaid taffeta dress and panties in red and cream, under a brass-buttoned red cloth coat, velvety leopard pattern muff and pill-box hat, socks, black snap-front velvet shoes, and she is carrying a red and gold cardboard hat box. The costume is tagged Binnie Walker, Madame Alexander, and the doll is preserved in her original box stamped Binnie and 1525. Near mint condition, beautiful complexion, coiffure, bright fresh costume and accessories. Alexander, Binnie Walker, model #1525, 1954. $500/800

18. Winsome Winnie Walker Variation from the 1954 Catalog

18" (46 cm.) All hard plastic, socket head, five piece walking style body, burly blonde hair with bangs, blue sleep eyes. Costume: a "swishy taffeta dress" (1954 catalog) in white under a stylish red taffeta coat with white pique collar and cuffs and having a matching white pique cap with red ribbons, panties, socks, black snap-front shoes, and carrying a black and gold hat box with brass Fashion Award medal. The costume is tagged Madame Alexander, New York, and is a slight fabric variation of the model shown in the 1954 catalog which described the doll as "Madame Alexander's newest walking doll. Great appeal has been captured in her little girl features". Near mint condition, beautiful complexion and blush, perfect coiffure and crisp fresh costume, with original box stamped Winnie Walker and 1836, and with a booklet showing 15 pages of additional costumes for her. Alexander, Winnie Walker, 1954. $500/800

20. "Winsome Binnie Walker, Pert and Gay", 1954

18" (46 cm.) All hard plastic, socket head, five piece walking style body, blue sleep eyes, blonde hair with bangs and original curls. Costume: black and white striped polished cotton dress with puffed sleeves under a yellow polished cotton pinafore with shoulder bows, straw bonnet with black and white striped band and bows, panties, socks, black velvet snap-front shoes, and carrying a black and gold hat box, with original box stamped "Binnie" and 1825, with original price tag of $13.98. The costume is tagged "Binnie Walker, Madame Alexander". Near mint condition, beautiful complexion and rich full original curls, vibrant and crisp original costume and accessories. Alexander, model #1825, the doll appeared in the 1954 catalog described as "pert and gay". $700/900

21. Annabelle Inspired by Kate Smith Stories with Fashion Award Brass Tag, 1952

15" (38 cm.) All hard plastic, socket head, five piece hard plastic body, large blue sleep eyes, blonde hair with bangs, the sides of hair swept away from her face and captured in a pink bow at the crown with curls below. Costume: pink cotton pique dress with pink rick-rack trim, under a knit turquoise sweater embroidered Annabelle in pink lettering, white cotton petticoat and panties, socks, black leatherette side-snap shoes, brass Fashion Award wrist tag, and presented in her original box stamped Annabelle and 1810, and having applied Fashion Award emblem. The costume is tagged Kate Smith's Annabelle, Madame Alexander, and on the inside petticoat is an original label from the famous department store Strawbridge and Clothier with a price tag of $11.98. Near mint condition, gorgeous complexion and perfectly-kept hair and costume. Alexander, Annabelle, 1952, the model was made for one year only, inspired by the stores of Annabelle written by the beloved television performer Kate Smith. $700/1000

Mary Martin and having a store tag of F.A.O. Schwarz. Near mint condition, beautiful complexion and full fluffy hair, small faint smudge above the red lettering on middy top, costume appears never removed from doll. Alexander, the doll was presented in 1949 and 1950 to coincide with the Broadway play, South Pacific, in which Mary Martin starred. $800/1000

23. Mary Martin in Ball Gown Costume with Fashion Award tag, 1950

15" (38 cm.) All hard plastic, socket head, blue sleep eyes, soft fleecy wig in light brown shaded color, five piece body. Costume: white sheer nylon gown with puffed sleeves, Peter Pan collar, red velvet ribbon bows, taffeta petticoat and panties, red front-snap shoes, and having paper Fashion Award tag and in original box stamped "Mary Martin". The costume is tagged "Madame Alexander New York". The doll represents Mary Martin in a costume from the Broadway play, South Pacific, in which she starred. Near mint condition, beautiful complexion and lush hair, pristine original costume. Alexander, 1950, the doll was made for only one year. $600/800

24. Unique Model Sleeping Beauty in Grand Size for Walt Disney, 1959

21" (53 cm.) Hard plastic socket head, hard plastic torso and legs that are jointed at hips and above the knees, high-heel feet, vinyl arms with elegant fingers, blue sleep eyes, very full lips, blonde hair with bangs and curls. Costume: rich sky blue satin gown with lady-fitted bodice, Juliette sleeves, gold metallic trim, petticoat, panties, stockings, gold sling heels, "diamond" necklace and ring, lavish gold metallic double-tiered crown studded with "diamonds, and full-length tulle cape with brocade pattern of silver and gold metallic threads. The costume is

22. Mary Martin in Sailor Costume from South Pacific, 1949

18" (46 cm.) All hard plastic, socket head, large brown eyes, five piece hard plastic body, brunette curly fleeced wig. Costume: sailor suit with middy top and black ribbon trim, embroidered Mary Martin in red, with sailor cap, white socks, black leatherette side-snap shoes. The costume is tagged Mary Martin of South Pacific, Madame Alexander, and the doll has an original paper clover leaf wrist tag, and its original box labeled

labeled "Madame Alexander presents Walt Disney's Sleeping Beauty", and the doll has a custom gold paper wrist label, and is presented in her original box stamped Sleeping Beauty, model 2195 (the actual doll measures 18" although the Alexander catalog described the doll as 21", presumably including her crown). Near mint condition, superb painting and preservation of complexion and features, original coiffure, impeccable costume with crisp vibrant colors and accessories. Alexander, 1959, for Walt Disney, the unique facial model model was used only for the two sizes of Sleeping Beauty and the 1960 model of Queen Elizabeth II. $1200/1500

25. Sleeping Beauty for Walt Disney with Unique Facial Model, Medium Size, 1959

16" (41 cm.) Hard plastic socket head, hard plastic torso and legs that are jointed at the hips and above the knees, high heel feet, vinyl arms, blue sleep eyes, blonde hair with curls and bangs. She is wearing the identical costume to #24 yet of a lighter color blue. The costume is tagged "Madame Alexander presents Walt Disney's Sleeping Beauty", and the doll wears her original custom designed paper wrist tag and is in her original box stamped Sleeping Beauty, and model #1895. (Note: the actual doll measures 15", although Alexander advertised the doll as being 16 1/2", presumably including the crown). Near mint condition, superb coloring and perfectly preserved coiffure and costume. Alexander for Walt Disney, 1959, with unique facial modeling. The costume was described in the catalog as "her golden tiara is slyly kissed with rhinestone stars". $500/800

26. Queen Elizabeth from the Beaux Arts Creations, Version #2020A, 1953

18" (46 cm.) All hard plastic, socket head, five piece walking-style body, dark blue sleep eyes, brunette hair in an elaborate arrangement of curls still affixed with original hair pins. Costume: ivory satin brocade gown with fitted lady bodice, blue silk sash with rhinestones, rubies and other jewels, hooped petticoat, panties, white stockings, snap shoes, and having silver crown set with faux-diamonds, faux-diamond earrings and bracelets. The costume is labeled Madame Alexander New York, and the doll is presented in her original box stamped Queen Elizabeth and model 2020A (which was the version without cape). Near mint condition, superb complexion and painting, perfect coiffure and costume, all accessories complete. Alexander, 1953 from the Beaux Arts Creations series. $1100/1500

27. Cissy Model of Queen Elizabeth, 1955

20" (51 cm.) Hard plastic socket head, hard plastic adult lady torso and legs that are jointed at the hips and knees and designed for wearing high heels, vinyl arms with shoulder and elbow jointing, blue/green sleep eyes, brunette hair pulled into a coronet at the crown and a flared chignon at the nape (still captured with original hairpins and net. Costume: ivory brocade gown with dart-shaped bodice, blue taffeta sash decorated with rhinestones and ruby, elbow-length gloves, petticoat, panties, stockings, sling heels, and having original silver metallic crown with imbedded rubies, pearl necklace and earrings, diamond ring, and jewel-studded bracelets. The costume is labeled Cissy, Madame Alexander, and she carries her original wrist tag. Excellent condition, the slightest surface dust on sash and gloves. Alexander, the premiere year of Cissy, 1955 was highlighted by this presentation of Queen Elizabeth in the series entitled "A Child's Dream Come True". $700/900

28. Queen Elizabeth from Beaux Arts Creations Model 2025 with Purple Robe, 1953

18" (46 cm.) All hard plastic, socket head, five-piece walking-style body, blue sleep eyes, brunette hair in original elaborate coiffure brushed away from face into arranged curls. Costume: ivory taffeta brocade with blue silk banner decorated with faux-diamonds, pearls, and ruby, petticoat, panties, stockings. shoes, silver metal crown, elaborate earrings and diamonds heavily encrusted with faux-diamonds and jewels. elbow-length gloves, rare purple velvet formal robe with "ermine" edging and gold metallic trim, and brass embossed Fashion Award wrist tag. Her costume is tagged Madame Alexander New York, and she is presented in her original box, model 2025. Beautiful condition with perfect original coiffure still captured with original hairpins, lovely complexion and fresh costume. Alexander, Queen Elizabeth II, from the Beaux Arts Creations series of 1953, this being the rarer model with purple velvet robe. $1200/1700

29. Cissette as Queen Elizabeth II, 1957

10" (25 cm.) All hard plastic with socket head, adult lady body with bendable knees, dark blue sleep eyes, ash blonde hair with side-part and slight forehead bangs. Costume: gold patterned taffeta brocade gown with flared fit and sleeveless straps, narrow blue banner with "jewel" trim, petticoat with lace ruffle, panties, stockings, sling heels, and having an elaborate gilt metallic crown with five large faux-diamonds, three-diamond earrings, pearl necklace, bracelet, original paper wrist tag. The doll is presented in her original box from

F.A.O. Schwarz, and the costume is tagged Cissette, Madame Alexander. Pristine condition with beautiful complexion, perfect coiffure and costume. Alexander, model #971, 1957. $400/600

30. Alexander-Kins as Queen from 1955 Catalog

8" (20 cm.) All hard plastic with straight leg walking style body, socket head, dark blue eyes, short dark blonde hair with flip curls and bangs. Costume: ivory taffeta brocade gown with scooped neck, fitted waist and full skirt, blue banner with faux-jewels, petticoat and panties with lace ruffles, gold shoes, silver crown with five silver medallions centering large faux-diamonds, pearl necklace, faux-diamond bracelet, and red velvet robe with gold metallic trim. The costume is tagged Alexander-Kins, Madame Alexander, she has an original wrist tag and her original box labeled Queen 499. Near mint condition with pristine coiffure, complexion and costume, a blue ribbon award winner from 1984 Alexander doll convention. Alexander, 1955. $400/600

31. Cissette "Dressed as a Queen" from 1958 Catalog

10" (25 cm.) All hard plastic with socket head, adult lady body with bendable knees, dark blue eyes, ash-blonde hair in original side-part coiffure with delicate bangs. She is wearing gold taffeta brocade gown with square-cut neckline and pouf sleeves, wide blue sash with faux-jewels, yellow taffeta petticoat with ruffle, lace-edged panties, stockings, gold sling heels, gold metallic crown set with faux-diamonds, "diamond" earrings and bracelet. The costume is tagged Cissette and she is in her original labeled box. Pristine original condition of coiffure, complexion and costume. Alexander, the doll appeared in the 1958 catalog, model #879, described as "Cissette dressed as a Queen". $400/600

32. Cissette as Queen from the 1962 Catalog

10" (25 cm.) All hard plastic with socket head, adult lady body with bendable knees, dark blue sleep eyes, dark blonde hair in center-part style with slight forehead bangs and flip curls. Costume: ivory taffeta gown with flocked metallic design and rhinestone appliques, blue silk sash with "jewel" trims, petticoat, panties, stockings, sling heels, gold metallic crown with "ruby" center and four faux-diamonds, pearl necklace, faux-diamond earrings and bracelet. The costume is labeled Madame Alexander and the doll has her original booklet and box marked Queen 763. Pristine condition with beautiful complexion, coiffure, and costume. $400/600

33. Cissette as Queen from 1963 Catalog

10" (25 cm.) All hard plastic, socket head, adult lady body with bendable knees, dark blue eyes, ash blonde center-parted hair with curls at each side of forehead. Costume: ivory taffeta brocade gown with gilded floral pattern and applique rhinestones, blue silk like sash with "jewels", taffeta petticoat, panties, stockings, sling heels, metal crown with very rich gilding and having a center "ruby" flanked by two faux-diamonds on each side, faux-diamond earrings and bracelets, pearl necklace. The costume is labeled Madame Alexander, and she has an original wrist booklet and box labeled 842 with original price of $8.95. Pristine condition with superb complexion, coiffure and costume, especially fine detail of crown and jewelry. Alexander, model #842 from their 1963 catalog. $400/600

34. Margot Ballerina in Pink Tutu with Binnie-Face Variant, 1956

15" (38 cm.) All hard plastic, socket head, bendable knees, blue eyes, dark eye shadow, ash blonde hair with rolled bangs and hair drawn away from face into an arranged curled ponytail at the back of her head. Costume: pale pink tutu with taffeta faille bodice, and multi-tiered ruffed skirt and straps, stockings, flat shoes, two rosebuds at the waist and one on the shoulder. The costume is labeled Madame Alexander and she has an original gold wrist booklet and original box labeled 1580. Near mint condition, superb complexion, coiffure and costume in crisp fresh colors. Alexander, the doll is shown in the Alexander catalog of 1956, model #1580, named Margot Ballerina, although her face model shown in the catalog and on this doll is that of Binnie. $700/1000

35. Alexander-Kins Ballerina from 1953 Catalog

7.5" (19 cm.) All hard plastic with socket head, five piece body with non-walking straight legs, dark sleep eyes, brunette hair with double-sewn center part, shot bangs, flip curls with little flowers. Costume: pink tutu with satin bodice trimmed with three rhinestones, matching panties, pink tulle skirt and sleeves, peach satin shoes with ribbon bows. The costume is labeled Alexander-Kins and she has a book-shaped original wrist tag, and original box labeled "Brunette 309". Pristine condition, perfect coiffure, fine satiny complexion, crisp costume. Alexander, the doll appeared in the 1953 catalog, the inaugural year of that model. $500/800

36. Alexander-Kins Girl in Pink Cotton Playsuit and Pinafore from 1953 Catalog

7.5" (19 cm.) All hard plastic with socket head, five piece non-walking body, dark blue eyes, dark ash blonde hair with bangs and flip curls. Costume: pink cotton one-piece romper suit with white rick-rack trim and a matching wide-brimmed sunbonnet, with flowered cotton pinafore, socks, side-snap shoes. The costume is marked Alexander-Kins and she has her original book-shaped wrist tag and is in original box labeled "Tosca". Pristine condition with nicely blushed complexion, perfect coiffure, crisp costume. Alexander, the doll appeared in the premiere year of Alexander-Kins production, 1953. $500/700

37. Alexander-Kins in Pink Checkered Play Set from 1953

7.5" (19 cm.) All hard plastic with socket head, five piece body with non-walking style legs, dark eyes, dark brunette hair with bangs and flip curls. Costume: pink and white checkered play suit with lace trim, matching sunbonnet with wide brim, matching gathered skirt, socks, black velvet side-snap shoes. The costume is tagged Alexander-Kins, the doll has her original book-shaped wrist tag, and is preserved in her original box labeled "brown" with Bullock's store label and price of $2.25. Alexander, 1953, from the premiere offering of the beloved Wendy model. $500/700

38. Alexander-Kins in Striped Green Pinafore Dress from 1953

7.5" (19 cm.) All hard plastic, socket head, five piece non-walking style body, blue/green eyes, brunette hair with bangs and curls. Costume: striped green/black and cream cotton pinafore dress with lime green rick-rack trim over matching panties with attached white organdy lace-edged blouse, socks, side-snap shoes, and stiffed lace bonnet with open back. The costume is labeled Alexander-Kins, the doll has her original book-shaped wrist booklet and she is preserved in her original box labeled "319 Brunette". Near mint condition with bright rosy cheeks, perfect coiffure and crisp fresh costume. Alexander, the premiere year of this model, 1953. $500/700

39. Alexander-Kins "Southern Girl" from 1953

7.5" (19 cm.) All hard plastic with socket head, five piece body with non-walking style legs, dark blue eyes, ash blonde hair with bangs and flip curls. Costume: peach/pink organdy dress with tucks and lace trim, taffeta petticoat and pantalets, straw bonnet with wide front brim and upturned back brim and feather and flower trim, socks, shoes. The costume is labeled Alexander-Kins and she has her original book-shaped wrist tag and is original box stamped "Southern Girl 305". Pristine condition with beautiful complexion and cheeks, perfect coiffure and crisp fresh costume. Alexander, the model appeared in their 1953 catalog, the premiere year of Alexander-Kins. $500/800

40. Alexander-Kins in White Organdy Party Dress from 1953

7.5" (19 cm.) All hard plastic, socket head, five piece non-walking style body, dark sleep eyes, ash-blonde hair with bangs and flip curls. Costume: white organdy party dress with lace trim at the neckline and sleeves, narrow ribbon borders, pink sash, lace-edged petticoat and panties, socks, side-snap shoes. The costume is labeled Alexander-Kins, the doll has her original book-shaped wrist booklet and is preserved in her original box labeled "tosca 549". Near mint, beautiful complexion with rosy cheeks, perfect coiffure and crisp fresh costume. $500/800

41. Cissy in "Long-Stemmed Gown of Black Velvet" from 1956

20" (51 cm.) Hard plastic socket head, hard plastic torso with adult lady modeling and legs with jointing at hips and knees, high-heel shaped feet, vinyl arms with elbow-jointing, green/blue sleep eyes, reddish-brown hair arranged in elaborate coiffure with short bangs, curls at crown and nape. Costume: black velvet tightly fitted evening gown with tulle lower skirt, flared decolletage lined with pink satin, clusters of roses at the hips and inside collar, black satin petticoat and panties, stockings, black sling heels with pink inner soles, faux-diamond earrings, bracelets and ring, pearl necklace. The costume is labeled Cissy, Madame Alexander, and the doll has original wrist booklet and original box labeled #2043. Near mint condition with perfectly preserved coiffure having original hairpins, lovely complexion, vibrant fresh costume and accessories. Alexander, Cissy, model 2043, appeared in the Alexander catalog of 1956 described as "a gown of great elegance on a beautiful doll". $1100/1500

42. Cissy as "The Lady in Red" from 1958 Catalog

20" (51 cm.) Hard plastic socket head, hard plastic adult lady-shaped torso and legs with hip and knee jointing, vinyl arms with elbow jointing, blue/green sleep eyes, ash-blonde hair in very elaborate coiffure. Costume: "holly-berry red taffeta cut skillfully with great wide skirt sweeping to the floor...and a sheer front of tulle stole with irridescent dots" (as described in Alexander catalog of 1958), white taffeta petticoat, panties, stockings, silver sling heels, pearl drop earrings, double-strand pearl necklace, faux-diamond ring and rhinestone waist brooch. The costume is labeled Cissy, Madame Alexander, she has her original wrist booklet and original box labeled #2285. Neat mint condition, the exceptional coiffure retains its pure original condition, beautiful complexion and vibrant costume colors. Alexander, model #2285, 1958, the doll was described in that year's catalog as The Lady in Red. $1200/1600

43. Cissy in Lingerie, 1956

20" (51 cm.) Hard plastic socket head, hard plastic torso with adult lady-shape and legs with jointing at hips and knees, vinyl arms with elbow jointing, blue-green sleep eyes, reddish-brown hair with short curled bangs and her hair pulled back and clasped by barrette at crown and then smoothed into curls at the nape. Costume: lacy chemise, stockings, lace-decorated high heel mules, pink nylon full-length peignoir with lace and pink ribbons edging the bodice, pearls, faux-diamond ring. The costume is labeled Cissy, Alexander, the doll has original wrist booklet, and she is preserved in her original box labeled 2100. near mint condition, perfectly-preserved coiffure, beautiful complexion, fresh and dainty costume. Alexander, Cissy, 1956, model 2100, "Basic Cissy" described as wearing "chemise of nylon lace, long nylon hose, and mules trimmed with lace and flowers"; the peignoir could be purchased separately. $800/1000

44. Cissette in Lilac Taffeta Dinner Dress, from 1957

10" (25 cm.) All hard plastic with socket head, adult lady-shaped body with bendable knees, high-heel-shaped feet, dark blue eyes, ash-blonde hair in original coiffure with soft forehead curls and gathered curls at the nape. Costume: lilac taffeta dinner dress with removable jacket and bouffant skirt, panties, stockings, lilac sling heels, lilac woven hair trimmed with violets and lavender flowers that match corsage on dress and applique flower on straw purse, faux-diamond earrings, pearl necklace. The costume is labeled Cissette, Madame Alexander, and the doll is preserved in original box labeled #943. Pristine condition, beautiful rosy cheeks and complexion, perfect original coiffure, vibrant fresh original costume. The doll appeared in the 1957 Alexander catalog, and is a near match to the Cissy model 2043 of the same year. $500/800

45. Brown-eyed Cissy in Lilac Taffeta Afternoon Ensemble from 1957 Catalog

20" (51 cm.) Hard plastic socket head, hard plastic torso with adult-lady shape and legs with jointing at hips and knees, feet posed for high heels, vinyl arms with elbow jointing, brown sleep eyes, ash-blonde hair in elaborate original coiffure with curls at the forehead, crown and nape. Costume: crisp lilac taffeta cocktail dress with triple-box-pleated full skirt, short sleeves, matching jacket with flared lapels, pink taffeta petticoat with tulle ruffles, panties, stockings, sling strap heels, lilac woven bonnet decorated with sprigs of lilacs and pale blue lily of the valley to match dress flowers, straw purse with berries, faux-diamond earrings, bracelet and ring, pearl necklace. The costume is labeled Cissy, Madame Alexander, she has an original wrist booklet, and original box marked 2143. Pristine condition with exceptionally beautiful complexion, perfectly preserved coiffure, vibrant and crisp costume. Alexander, model #2143 from 1957 catalog. The costume is nearly identical to #45 Cissette. $1200/1600

46. Alexander-Kins as Bridesmaid in PInk Tulle from 1955

8" (20 cm.) All hard plastic with one-piece walking style legs, socket head, dark blue eyes, painted lower lashes, ash-blonde double-seamed hair with arranged curls and bangs. Costume: "great flaring gown of petal pink nylon tulle, trimmed with flowers" (1955 catalog description . With leaf-shaped cap sprinkled with tiny flowers, panties, peach satin shoes with pink bows. The costume is labeled Alexander-Kins and she is in her original box labeled Bridesmaid 478. Near mint condition, very beautiful blush and complexion, flawless coiffure and superb freshness of costume. Alexander, the doll was presented in the 1955 catalog named "Wendy's Bridesmaid". $400/600

47. Alexander-Kins "Wendy Makes a Beautiful Bride" from 1955

9" (23 cm.) All hard plastic with one-piece walking-style legs, socket head, dark blue sleep eyes, painted lower lashes, auburn hair. Costume: "gown of heavy white satin, Juliet cap of lace and nylon tulle bridal veil" as described in 1955 Alexander catalog; the gown trimmed with torchon lace at the yoke, lace-edged taffeta petticoat and panties, garter, peach satin shoes with ivory bows, floral bouquet to match flowers on cap. The costume is labeled Alexander-Kins and she is preserved in her original box labeled Bride 475 and auburn. Pristine condition with perfectly preserved coiffure, complexion and costume. Alexander, described as "Wendy makes a beautiful bride" in the 1955 Alexander catalog. $400/600

48. Alexander-Kins in Pink Taffeta Party Dress from 1954

8" (20 cm.) All hard plastic with one-piece walking-style legs, socket head, dark blue sleep eyes, painted lower lashes, blonde hair with curly bangs and flip curls. Costume: crisp pink taffeta dress with lace edging, flower at waist, matching panties and hair bow, socks, side-snap velvet shoes. The costume is labeled Alexander-Kins and the doll has her original book-shaped wrist tag, and is her original box labeled 510 Blonde. Near mint condition, perfectly preserved coiffure, bright rosy cheeks, crisp and fresh costume. Alexander, 1954. $400/500

49. Alexander-Kins "Vistor's Day at School" from 1955 Catalog

8" (20 cm.) All hard plastic with one-piece walking-style legs, socket head,

dark blue sleep eyes, painted lower lashes, blonde hair with curly bangs and flip curls. Costume: aqua polished cotton dress under a cotton pinafore of tiny pink and white checkered design with lace edging, lace-edged cotton petticoat, panties, socks, pink velvet side-snap shoes, woven straw bonnet with border of roses and leaves. The costume is labeled Alexander-Kins, she has her original book-shaped wrist booklet, and is preserved in her original box marked 450 blonde. Near mint condition, perfectly preserved coiffure and costume, lovely costume with bright rosy cheeks. Alexander, the doll appeared in the 1955 catalog described as "Wendy dresses for visitor's day at school". $400/600

50. Alexander-Kins "Plane Trip" from 1955 Catalog

8" (20 cm.) All hard plastic with one-piece walking-style legs, socket head, blue sleep eyes, painted lower lashes, tosca hair with curly bangs and flip curls. Costume: navy blue flannel jacket with silver buttons over polished cotton dress with Peter Pan collar, cut-work trimmed petticoat, lace-edged panties, socks, red velvet side-snap shoes, felt beanie cap with two red pom-poms. The costume is labeled Alexander-Kins and she is preserved in her original box labeled 452 Tosca. Near mint condition, beautiful cheek color and coiffure, perfectly preserved costume except one snap cover missing. Alexander, the doll appeared in the 1955 catalog described as "Wendy wearing an outfit she like for a plane trip". $300/500

51. Red-Haired Alexander-Kins as "Madeline", F.A.O. Schwarz Exclusive, 1953

8" (20 cm.) All hard plastic with five-piece walking-style body, socket head, dark sleep eyes, double-seamed auburn wig in unusual side-parted style with red ribbon bow. Costume: blue charmbray demin tunic with red, white and blue striped edging on double pockets, over a sleeveless jump suit with chambray pants and red and white striped cotton top, white socks, red velvet side-snap shoes. The costume is labeled Madeline by Madame Alexander, and the doll is preserved in her original box labeled Madeline. Pristine condition with superb coiffure, beautiful rosy complexion, and crisp fresh original costume. Alexander, 1953/54, the doll was

sold as petite companion to the fully-jointed 18" Madeline who was also offered in a matching costume, exclusively for F.A.O. Schwarz in that year. $700/900

52. Elise Bride in Richly Embroidered Tulle Gown, 1958

17" (43 cm.) Hard plastic socket head, hard plastic torso with adult-lady shape, and legs with jointing at hips, knees and ankles, vinyl arms with elbow jointing, blue sleep eyes, brunette hair with original coiffure, rolled bangs, scalloped waves around the sides of her face and pinned pageboy curls at the nape (held in original net). Costume: very flouncy white tulle gown with attached shoulder drape, scalloped hem, and lavish bridal wreath design embroidery, over organdy underskirt, taffeta petticoat and panties, stockings, silver sling heels, elaborate floral coronet with floor-length veil, bouquet of wedding flowers, pearl drop earrings, pearl necklace and bracelet, faux-diamond solitaire ring. The costume is labeled Elise, Madame Alexander, she has her original wrist booklet and she is preserved in her original box labeled 1750. Pristine condition with superb complexion, coiffure, and costume. Alexander, Elise, the doll appeared in the 1958 catalog described as "wearing a gown of great elegance". $600/900

52.1. Cissette Bride in Matching Wedding Ensemble from 1958

10" (25 cm.) All hard plastic with socket head, adult-lady shaped torso, jointing at shoulders, hips and knees, high-heel feet, blue sleep eyes, ash-blonde hair with bangs and flip curls. Costume: tulle gown with draped collar over fitted bodice, billowing tulle skirt with rich bridal wreath medallion embroidery, coronet of flowers with attached veil, matching bouquet, organdy underskirt, taffeta petticoat and panties, stockings, silver sling heels, pearl earrings and necklace. The costume is labeled Cissette, Madame Alexander, and the doll is preserved in her original box labeled 876. Near mint condition with especially

lovely complexion. Alexander, the bride appeared in the 1958 catalog, a complementary model to the larger Cissy bride of the same year. $500/800

53. Elise Bride in "Triumphantly Feminine" Pink Gown from 1959

17" (43 cm.) Hard plastic socket head, hard plastic lady-shaped body and legs with jointing at hips, knees and ankles, vinyl arms with jointed elbows, blue sleep eyes, auburn hair with soft curly bangs, scallop-waved hair away from face into pageboy roll at the nape, Costume: pale pink tulle gown with billowing pleated skirt, wide pouf sleeves with lace frills that are repeated at the bodice, pink silk-like sash that forms into a large bow at the back, pink organdy underskirt, pink taffeta petticoat and panties, stockings, pink sling heels, coronet of pink-tipped flowers and leaves with full-length pink tulle veil, faux-diamond earrings and solitaire ring. The costume is labeled Elise, Madame Alexander, and she has her original paper wrist label. Near mint condition with exquisite complexion and blush, superbly preserved coiffure and costume. Alexander, the model #1835, appeared in the Alexander catalog of 1959, shown here in very rare pink color variation. $800/1100

54. Elise Bride "Triumphantly Feminine" Traditional Gown from 1959

17" (43 cm.) Hard plastic socket head, hard plastic lady-shaped torso and legs with jointed hips, knees and ankles, vinyl arms with elbow-jointing, blue sleep eyes, blonde hair with curly bangs, scalloped waves around the sides of face and captured in pageboy curls at the nape. Costume: an identical gown to #53 except of ivory color, with floral variation in the coronet and bouquet, with original undergarments, shoes, jewelry. The costume is labeled Elise, Madame Alexander, the doll wears her original wrist booklet, and is preserved in her original box. Beautiful condition with pristine coiffure and complexion. Alexander, the doll appeared in the 1959 catalog with the description "Nothing is so triumphantly feminine as a bride." $600/800

55. Elise Bride of "Softest White Satin" from 1960 Catalog

17" (43 cm.) Hard plastic socket head, hard plastic lady-shaped torso and legs with jointing at hips, knees and ankles, vinyl arms with elbow jointing, blue sleep eyes, dark brunette hair with forehead curls above scalloped-edge hair drawn back at the sides into a pageboy at the back. Costume: rich white satin gown "fully lined to give it body" with bodice decorated with sequins and crystal beads and a "wide satin cascade" at the back that "falls gracefully to the floor", with flowing veil from coronet of orange blossoms and lilies of the valley and matching bridal bouquet, tulle stiffened taffeta petticoat, panties, stockings, silver sling heels, pearl earrings and necklace, faux-diamond solitaire ring. The costume is labeled Elise, Madame Alexander, and she has her original wrist booklet and box labeled Elise 1735. Near mint condition, beautiful complexion with soft blush, perfect coiffure and costume. Alexander, the bride appeared in the 1960 catalog, model 1730. $700/1000

56. Cissette in Black Velvet Formal Gown from 1957

10" (25 cm.) Hard plastic socket head, all hard plastic body with adult-lady shaped torso and jointing at hips, knees, and shoulders, dark blue sleep eyes, ash-blonde double-seamed hair with two curls onto forehead, hair drawn away from face into chignon at crown and nape. Costume: black velvet full-length strapless gown with jet beading at the bodice, pink taffeta ruffled petticoat and panties, stockings, black sling heels, faux-fur stole with sweetheart roses, faux-diamond earrings and bracelet. The costume is labeled Cissette, Madame Alexander and the doll is preserved in her original box labeled 973. Excellent condition with perfectly preserved coiffure, beautiful costume. Alexander, model 973 from the 1957 catalog described as a "fitted gown with a regal air". $400/500

57. Cissette in Green Velvet Formal Gown

10" (25 cm.) All hard plastic with socket head, adult lady-shaped torso, jointing at shoulders, knees and hips, sleep eyes, blonde hair with spit curls onto forehead and hair drawn back and held by a velvet bow at the crown and a loose cluster of curls at the nape. Costume: emerald green velvet full-length gown with dart-shaped fit, pink taffeta petticoat with lace ruffles and panties, stockings, gold sling heels, faux-fur stole with sweetheart roses, faux-diamond earrings and bracelet. The costume is labeled Cissette, Madame Alexander and she is preserved with original wrist booklet in her original box labeled 872. Near mint condition with beautifully blushed cheeks, perfect coiffure, crisp and fresh costumes. Alexander, the costume is similar to model #973, c. 1957. $500/700

58. Cissette as "Small Elegance" from 1958 Catalog

10" (25 cm.) All hard plastic with socket head, adult lady-shaped torso, jointing at shoulders, knees and hips, sleep eyes, brunette hair with spit curls onto forehead, her hair drawn back into a cluster of curls at her crown decorated with sweetheart roses and arranged curls at her nape. Costume: ivory silk ball gown printed with shaded flowers and leaves, fitted bodice with dainty self-bow at the waist, rose velvet stole lined with matching silk fabric, ivory taffeta petticoat with tulle edging, panties, stockings, gold sling heels, pearl earrings. The costume is labeled Cissette, Madame Alexander, and he is presented in her original box labeled 873. Near mint conditiion, very beautiful complexion and coiffure, perfectly preserved costume. Alexander, the doll appeared in the 1958 catalog described as "small elegance...she is irresistable". $600/900

59. Cissette in "Ruffles and Rosebuds", 1961 Catalog

10" (25 cm.) All hard plastic, socket head, adult lady-shaped torso, jointed shoulders, hips and knees, sleep eyes, blonde hair with rolled bangs and an elaborate cluster of arranged curls at the crown and at the nape of neck. Costume: full-length party gown of elaborately tiered tulle ruffles accented with rosebuds and rhinestones, rose silk sash with long bow at the back waist, faux-diamond earrings and bracelet, pink taffeta petticoat and panties, stockings, gold sling heels. The costume is labeled Cissette and she is preserved in her original box labeled 831. Near mint, very beautiful complexion and superb coiffure, excellent costume. Alexander, the doll appeared in the 1961 catalog described as "ruffles and rosebuds". $400/600

60. Cissette in "Yard and Yards of Ruffles" Gown from 1962

10" (25 cm.) All hard plastic, socket head, adult lady-shaped torso, jointing at shoulders, hips and knees, sleep eyes, blonde hair with bangs, elaborately arranged curls at the crown and nape. Costume: pink tulle with an extravagant arrangement of ruffles overall the skirt and around the neckline, patterned pink sash, rosebud appliques, pink taffeta petticoat, panties, stockings, gold sling heels, large faux-diamond earrings and bracelet. The costume is labeled Cissette, Madame Alexander, and she has her original wrist booklet and is presented in her original box labeled 745. Near mint condition, superb complexion and coiffure, crisp and fresh costume. Alexander, the doll appeared as model 745 in the 1962 catalog described as having "a dance frock of nylon tulle with yards and yards of ruffles". $500/700

61. Cissy in Mauve Taffeta Gown from "A Child's Dream Come True" Series. 1955

20" (51 cm.) Hard plastic socket head, hard plastic torso with adult-lady shape and legs with jointing at hips and knees, high-heel shaped feet, vinyl arms with elbow jointing, brunette hair arranged with scalloped waves around the forehead, and then pulled into arranged curls at the crown and nape, blue/green sleep eyes. Costume: mauve taffeta sheath fitted gown with deep decolletage and widely flared skirt below her hips, trimmed with pearlized braid at the neckline and having a wide sash of aqua, gold and mauve with over-sized bow, mauve/pink taffeta and tulle petticoat, panties, stockings with one wide medallion-decorated garter, gold sling heels, pearl triple-tear drop earrings, double-band faux-diamond bracelet and solitaire ring. The costume is labeled Cissy, Madame Alexander and she has her original paper booklet and is preserved in her original box labeled Cissy 2100. Near mint condition, very beautiful complexion and perfect coiffure, crisp and fresh costume with original and unusual accessories. Alexander, 1955, model 2100, the doll appeared in the prestige series "A Child's Dream Come True" described in the catalog as "a very unusual gown". $1000/1400

62. Cissy in Aqua Taffeta from "Cissy Models her Formal Gown" Series, 1957

20" (51 cm.) Hard plastic socket head, hard plastic torso with adult-lady shape and legs jointed at hips and knees, high-heel shaped feet, vinyl arms with elbow joints, blue/green sleep eyes, auburn hair with side-curl bangs, and her hair waved back, clasped by a gold barette at the crown and captured into curls at the nape. Costume: crisp aqua taffeta full-length gown with low-cut bodice, double-pouf sleeves, decorated with aqua velvet sash and sweetheart roses that match the trim on her dyed to match wide-brimmed woven bonnet, lavender taffeta petticoat, panties, stockings, silver sling heels, faux-diamond drop earrings and solitaire ring, pearl bracelet. The costume is labeled Cissy, Madame Alexander, and she is preserved in her original box stamped Cissy 2176. Near mint condition, beautiful complexion, perfectly kept coiffure, and splendid crisp and fresh costume. Alexander, 1957, model 2176, the doll appeared in the "Cissy Models her Formal Gown" series described as "radiant in a gown of whispering taffeta". $1200/1600

63. Cissette Bride in Gossamer Tulle, 1957

10" (25 cm.) All hard plastic with socket head, adult-lady shaped torso, jointing at shoulders, hips and knees, high-heel-shaped feet, blue sleep eyes, double-seamed blonde hair with curly bangs and flip curls. Costume: wedding gown with white satin fitted bodice decorated with a drape of tulle at the neckline and having a very full fine tulle skirt over taffeta, panties, stockings, silver sling heels, tulle veil with coronet of pink and white flowers that match her bridal bouquet, pearl drop earrings, necklace and bracelet. The costume is labeled Cissette, Madame Alexander and she is preserved in her original box labeled Cissette, 970. Near mint condition, beautiful rosy complexion, perfect coiffure, bright fresh costume. Alexander, 1957, model 970, the doll was shown on the catalog cover that year described as "gowned and veiled in a haze of gossamer tulle". $400/600

64. Cissette Bride with Cascading Bridal Bouquet, 1960

10" (25 cm.) All hard plastic with socket head, adult-lady shaped torso, jointing at shoulders, hips and knees, high-heel-shaped feet, sleep eyes, shoulder-length blonde hair with curly bangs. Costume: white nylon tulle gown with long pleated full skirt over taffeta petticoat, panties, stockings, garter, silver sling heels, pearl necklace and earrings, tiny pearl buttons at sleeve edges, silk sash, cascading bridal bouquet of white roses and flowers that matches the very generous coronet with full-length tulle veil. The costume is labeled Cissette, Madame Alexander, and the doll has her original wrist booklet and box labeled 840. Near mint condition, perfectly kept coiffure, rosy cheeks, fresh costume with splendid bouquet and coronet. Alexander, model 840, 1960. $400/600

65. Cissette Bride with Sequin Coronet, 1961

10" (25 cm.) All hard plastic with socket head, adult-lady-shaped torso with jointing at shoulders, hips and knees, high-heel-shaped feet, sleep eyes, ash-blonde hair with curly bangs and flip curls. Costume: white tulle long-sleeved gown with dart-fitted bodice and very full skirt over organdy under-skirt, panties, stockings, garter, silver sling heels, pearl earrings, solitaire, and having a coronet of woven pearlized sequins that match trim on the gown neckline, tulle veil, and bridal bouquet of white flowers. The costume is labeled Cissette, Madame Alexander, and the doll has her original wrist booklet and box marked 840. Near mint condition, very beautiful complexion and coiffure, crisp and fresh costume. Alexander, model 840, 1961. $400/600

66. Cissette Bride with Lace Coronet, 1962

10" (25 cm.) All hard plastic with socket head, adult-lady shaped torso, jointing at hips, knees and shoulders, high-heel shaped feet, sleep eyes, shoulder-length blonde hair with curly bangs and flip curls. Costume: white tulle gown with wide border of lace trim at the hem to complement the wide lace collar, organdy petticoat, panties, stockings, garter, silver sling heels, pearl earrings, white flower bridal bouquet, crown-shaped lace coronet with rhinestone decorations and long tulle veil. The costume is tagged Cissette, Madame Alexander, and the doll has her original wrist booklet and box labeled 755. Near mint condition, bright rosy cheeks, perfect coiffure and costume. Alexander, model 7455, the doll was shown in the 1962 catalog

64.

65.

66.

67.

described as "looking demure and beautiful" and her costume was described as "frosted" with lace. $400/600

67. Cissette Bride with Lace Ruffled Gown, 1963

10" (25 cm.) All hard plastic with socket head, adult-lady shape torso, jointing at hips, knees and shoulders, high-heel shaped feet, blue sleep eyes, ash-blonde hair with curly bangs and flip curls. Costume: white tulle gown with three tiered of narrow lace ruffles on the bodice to match ruffles on skirt hem and cuffs, V-shaped satin sash, tulle underskirt, organdy petticoat, panties, stockings, silver sling heels, garter, wide coronet of pink and white flowers to match bridal bouquet, tulle veil, pearl earrings. The costume is labeled Cissette, Madame Alexander, and the doll is presented in her original box marked 755. Near mint condition with beautiful rosy cheeks, perfect coiffure and costume. Alexander, model 755, 1963. $400/600

66. Elise Bride "Looking Like a Dream" with New Hairdo, 1961

17" (43 cm.) Hard plastic socket head, hard plastic torso with adult-lady shape and legs with jointed hips, knees and ankles, vinyl arms with elbow joints, blue sleep eyes, dark brunette hair in cropped curly style with curls framing her face and cropped short at the back. Costume: white nylon tulle gown with pouf sleeves, double rows of tiny seed pearls at the neckline, gathered skirt with borders of floral tatting at the hem, neckline and cascading down the skirt, tulle underskirt, organdy petticoat, panties, stockings, garter, silver sling shoes, with floral coronet of blue and white flowers that matches her bridal bouquet, pearl earrings, solitaire and full length tulle veil, original wrist booklet and original box labeled Elise 1835. The costume is labeled Elise, Madame Alexander. near mint condition, superb complexion, perfectly preserved coiffure and costume. Alexander, 1961, model 1835 described in that year's catalog as "looking like a dream...her wig is new and most becoming".
$800/1200

69. Elise in Ball Gown of Cornflower Blue, 1960

17" (43 cm.) Hard plastic socket head, hard plastic torso with adult-lady shape and legs with jointing at hips, knees and ankles, vinyl arms with elbow jointing, blue sleep eyes, ash-blonde hair with rolled bangs and hair waved back into curls at the back of her head, decorated by a coronet of sweetheart roses that match the roses on her gown. Costume: cornflower blue tulle gown with fitted bodice and draping details, blue organdy petticoat, panties, stockings, silver sling heels, blue "sapphire" necklace, rhinestone earrings and solitaire ring. The costume is labeled Elise, Madame Alexander, and she is preserved in her original box labeled Elise 1730 with original store label from FAO Schwarz. Near mint condition with beautiful detail of costume and accessories. Alexander, model 1730, described in the 1960 catalog as wearing a gown of "cornflower blue". $600/900

70. Elise Bride "Looking Like a Dream" with Classic Hairdo, 1961

17" (43 cm.) Hard plastic socket head, hard plastic lady-shaped torso and legs with jointing at hips, knees and ankles, vinyl arms with jointing at elbows, blue sleep eyes, ash-blonde hair with spit curls, scalloped waves around the face and captured at the crown with a gold barette, forming into arranged curls at the nape. Costume: an identical tulle gown to doll #68, model 1835 with variations of flower colors, pearl earrings, solitaire, and with more traditional coiffure. The costume is labeled Elise, Madame Alexander, and the doll has her original wrist booklet and is presented in her original box labeled Elise 1835. Near mint condition, beautiful complexion and coiffure, perfect costume. Alexander, model 1835, 1961. $600/900

71. Elise as "Scarlett" from 1963

17" (43 cm.) Hard plastic socket head, hard plastic torso with adult-lady shape and legs with jointing at hips, knees and elbows, vinyl arms with elbow jointing, sleep eyes, dark brunette hair with curly bangs and long curly locks. Costume: full-length organdy gown trimmed with lace, tucks and rosebuds, taffeta and tulle petticoat, panties, stockings, silver sling heels, pearl earrings, solitaire, wide-brimmed woven bonnet with a circlet of roses. The costume is labeled Elise, Madame Alexander and the doll has her original wrist booklet and is in her original box labeled Scarlett Elise, 1750. Near mint, gorgeous complexion and coiffure, perfect costume with slight surface dust. Alexander, model 1750, the doll appeared in the 1963 catalog described as an "exquisite creation". $600/900

72. Elise as "Renoir" in Rose Taffeta, 1963

17" (43 cm.) Hard plastic socket head, hard plastic torso with adult-lady shape and legs with jointing at hips, knees and ankles, vinyl arms with elbow joints, sleep eyes, dark brunette hair with curly bangs and a gathered cluster of curls at her nape. Costume: rose taffeta gown with lace frills at the bodice, double ruffles at the skirt hem, black velvet ribbons and bows, white taffeta and tulle petticoat, panties, stockings, black sling heels, three-diamond earrings, cameo, solitaire, taffeta reticule with black lace and a splendid white woven bonnet decorated with a multitude of colorful flowers. The costume is labeled Elise, Madame Alexander and she has her original wrist booklet and box labeled Renoir Elise 1765. Near mint condition, gorgeous complexion and coiffure, perfect costume with crisp, fresh colors and fabrics. Alexander model 1765, the doll appeared in the 1963 catalog described as "looking exactly like a Renoir painting". $700/1000

with upturned brims and berry and flower trim, rhinestone circle earrings. The costume is labeled Alexander-Kins and the doll is presented in original box labeled Southern Belle with original $5.98 price label. Near mint condition. Alexander, 1956. $400/500

74. Alexander-Kins "Prince Charles of England", 1957

8" (20 cm.) All hard plastic with socket head, bendable knee walking-style body, sleep eyes, blonde side-parted flocked boy's hair. Costume: blue boy's suit with brass buttons, matching cap, white shirt, white socks and oxfords. The costume is labeled Alexander-Kins. Near mint condition, presented in original box labeled 397 Blonde. Alexander, model 397, 1957 described in that year's catalog as having 'great expectations" and named Prince Charles. $300/500

75. Alexander-Kins "First Communion", 1957

8" (20 cm.) All hard plastic with socket head, bendable-knee walking-style body, sleep eyes, brunette hair with bangs and flip curls. Costume: white organdy best dress with lace ruffles at hem and lace bretelles, silk ribbon streamers, organdy slip and panties, socks, tan velvet side-shape shoes, woven torchon lace cap with lilies of the valley and chapel veil, matching bouquet. The costume is labeled Alexander-Kins and the doll is presented in her original box labeled 395 Brown. Near mint condition, rosy cheeks, very fresh costume. Alexander, model 395 the model appeared on the cover of the 1957 catalog named "First Communion". $500/700

76. Alexander-Kins "Visits Grandma", 1965

8" (20 cm.) All hard plastic with socket head, bendable-knee walking-style body, sleep eyes, ash-blonde hair with bangs and flip curls. Costume: peach organdy best dress with five tiers of lace on the bodice and double lace tiers on skirt, matching petticoat, pink taffeta panties and hair bow, white socks, black velvet side-snap shoes. The costume is labeled Wendy-kins, the doll has original Wendy booklet and is preserved in her original box labeled Wendy-kins 621. Near mint condition, beautiful rosy cheeks, perfectly kept hair and costume. Alexander, model #621, the doll was described in the 1965 catalog as going "to visit Grandma". $400/500

73. Alexander-Kins as "Southern Belle", 1956

8" (20 cm.) All hard plastic with socket head, bendable knee walking-style body, sleep eyes, double-seamed ash-blonde hair in elaborately arranged curls. Costume: aqua and cream taffeta gown in the 1860 style, cut-work petticoat, pantalets, socks, black velvet side-snap shoes, black straw bonnet

77. Alexander-Kins as "Parlor Maid", 1956

8" (20 cm.) All hard plastic with socket head, bendable-knee walking-style body, sleep eyes, ash-blonde hair with bangs and flip curls. Costume: black taffeta dress with lace trim on sleeves to match the organdy apron trim, lace cap with black ribbons, scalloped-edge embroidered organdy petticoat and panties, white socks, black side-snap velvet shoes, with duster. The costume is labeled Alexander-kins and the doll is preserved in her original box labeled 579 Kins. Near mint, perfect kept coiffure, crisp and fresh costume, rosy cheeks. Alexander, model #579 from 1956 catalog described as "parlor maid looking very busy". $400/600

78. Alexander-Kins with "Oriental Influence", 1956

8" (20 cm.) All hard plastic, socket head, bendable-knee walking-style body, sleep eyes, ash-blonde hair with bangs and flip curls. Costume: mandarin-style woven straw bonnet and orange cotton coat with royal blue lining that matches her royal blue cotton dress and panties, socks, black side-snap velvet shoes. The costume is labeled Alexander-Kins, and the doll is presented in her original box labeled 591 tosca. Near mint condition, beautiful colors of complexion and costume, perfectly kept coiffure. Alexander, model #591, from 1956 catalog that described the "Oriental influence...mandarin coat and straw hat". $400/500

79. Alexander-Kins "Loves Going to the Circus", 1960

8" (20 cm.) All hard plastic, socket head, bendable-knee walking-style body, sleep eyes, blonde hair with bangs and braids tied with red silk ribbons. Costume: white pique blouse with attached red panties, black and white checkered pleated skirt with red waist-band, red collar bow, white socks, tan side-snap velvet shoes, red woven straw hat with black band. The costume is labeled Alexander-Kins and the doll is presented in her original box labeled Kins 332. Near mint condition, nice rosy cheeks. Alexander, model 332, described in the 1960 catalog as "Wendy loves going to the circus". $300/500

80. Alexander-Kins "Billy, the Boy Next Door", 1959

8" (20 cm.) All hard plastic, socket head, bendable-knee walking-style body, sleep eyes, blonde side-parted hair in flocked boyish style. Costume, one piece piece suit with white top, red shorts and striped waist-band, red brimmed cap, white socks, tan laced shoes. The costumed is labeled Alexander-Kins and the doll is in its original box labeled Kins 420. Excellent condition. Alexander, model #420, named "Billy the boy next door" in the 1959 catalog. $300/400

81. Cissy in "Red Taffeta", 1956

20" (51 cm.) Hard plastic socket head and adult lady-shaped torso and legs with jointing at hips and knees, vinyl arms with elbow joints, sleep eyes, very thick brunette shoulder-length hair with bangs and arranged curls. Costume: red taffeta dress with fitted bodice, slightly dropped waist, "rustly taffeta can-can petticoat", panties, stockings, black sling heels with unusually wide vamp, straw cloche with drape of white tulle trimmed with burgundy roses. The costume is labeled Cissy and the doll is presented in her original box labeled Cissy 2012. Near mint condition, beautiful rosy cheeks. Alexander, model #2012, the doll was presented in the 1956 catalog. $800/1200

82. Cissette in Red Faille Coat and Sheath, 1963

10" (25 cm.) All hard plastic with socket head, adult lady-shaped body, jointing at shoulders, hips and knees, high-heel shaped feet, sleep eyes, brunette hair in bouffant style. Costume: red faille sleeveless sheath with matching flared coat lined in white satin, panties, stockings, red sling heels, woven pillbox-style hat wrapped in a cloud of tulle and trimmed with a red rose, rhinestone earrings. The costume is labeled Madame Alexander and the doll has her original paper wrist booklet and is preserved in her original box labeled 748 with original FAO Schwarz store label. Near mint condition, bright rosy cheeks, perfectly preserved coiffure and costume. Alexander, model 748, the doll appeared in their 1953 catalog. $400/600

83. Cissy in "Garden Party" Ensemble, 1957

20" (51 cm.) Hard plastic socket head, adult lady-shaped torso and legs with jointing at hips and knees, vinyl arms with elbow-jointing, blue/green sleep eyes, ash-blonde hair with short curly bangs, the sides of her hair arranged in scallop waves at the sides of her forehead and captured with a barette at the crown and into arranged curls at the nape. Costume: crisp yellow taffeta dress with delicate floral print, fitted bodice, lace sleeve edges, black satin sash, pink lace petticoat, pink taffeta panties, stockings, black sling heels, black woven wide-brimmed bonnet trimmed with over-sized velvet roses, pearl earrings and double-strand bracelet, cameo, solitaire. The costume is labeled Cissy, the doll has her original wrist booklet, and is presented in original box. Near mint condition, gorgeous complexion, coiffure, and perfectly preserved fabulous costume. Alexander, model #2120, the costume described in the 1957 catalog as offering "ripples of rhythm as Cissy walks along". $1100/1500

53

84. Cissette "Sleeping Beauty" for Walt Disney, 1959

10" (25 cm.) All hard plastic with socket head, adult lady-shaped torso, jointing at shoulders, hips and knees, high-heel posed feet, sleep eyes, bright golden blonde hair. Costume: aqua taffeta gown with gold metallic net overlay bodice and extended robe, taffeta petticoat and panties, stockings. gold sling heels, gold crown with faux-diamond centered floral medallions. The costume is labeled Madame Alexander Presents Walt Disney's Sleeping Beauty, and her original gold custom wrist tag and box label are identified similarly. Near mint condition, gorgeous crisp costume and rosy complexion, perfect coiffure. Alexander, model #795, 1959, the smallest of the three models of Sleeping Beauty, the other two having unique facia models. $400/600

85. Cissette Ballerina in Aqua Tutu, 1960

10" (25 cm.) All hard plastic with socket head and adult lady-shaped torso, jointing at shoulders, hips and knees, high-heel shaped feet, sleep eyes, ash-blonde hair with bangs and arranged curls at the nape. Costume: aqua tutu with satin bodice and layers of gathered tulle skirt, attached satin panties, ballet slippers, coronet of flowers to match festoons on shoulder and waist, rhinestone earrings. The costume is labeled Cissette and the doll is presented in an Alexander box labeled 740. Near mint condition, beautiful rosy cheeks and crisp fresh costume and coiffure. Alexander, c. 1960. $300/500

86. Elise Ballerina in Gold Flecked Costume, 1959

17" (43 cm.) Hard plastic socket head, adult-lady shaped torso, and legs with jointing at hips, knees and ankles, vinyl arms with shoulder and elbow jointing, sleep eyes, ash-blonde hair with rolled bangs, side scallop-waved hair captured at crown with barette and having a cluster of curls at her nape. Costume: gold tutu with gold metallic bodice and pants under woven net skirt flecked with gold, sequin woven gold trim at the neckline and straps, waist, and forming an elaborate coronet, gold ballet slippers, rhinestone earrings. The costume appears in her original box labeled Elise 1810 with original price tag of $11.95. Near mint condition, gorgeous complexion, and perfectly preserved coiffure and costume. Alexander, model #1810, 1959, the costume was also presented for Cissette and Wendy during that same year, as shown here. $700/900

87. Cissette Ballerina in Gold-Flecked Costume, 1959

10" (25 cm.) All hard plastic with socket head, adult lady-shaped torso, jointing at shoulders, hips and knees, high-heel shaped feet, sleep eyes, ash-blonde hair with bangs and extended length curls at the nape. Costume: an identical costume to preceding Elise Ballerina except having pearl earrings and slightly less ornamental detail of coronet and without waist trim. The costume is labeled Cissette and the doll has her original wrist booklet and original box labeled 713. Near mint condition. Alexander, model #713, 1959 from the trilogy of matched ballerinas. $500/700

88. Alexander-Kins Ballerina in Gold-Flecked Costume, 1959

8" (20 cm.) All hard plastic with socket head, bendable-knee walking-style body, sleep eyes, ash-blonde hair with curly bangs and flip curls. Costume: identical to Elise and Cissette costumes (preceding) except having less detail of sequin trim on coronet and costume, and varying shoes. The costume has original Alexander-Kins label and the doll has original wrist booklet and appears in her original box labeled Ballerina 431. Near mint condition, perfectly preserved. Alexander, 1959, from the trilogy of matched ballerina costumes. $300/500

89. Elise Ballerina in Lilac Tutu, 1957

17" (43 cm.) Hard plastic socket head, adult-female shaped torso and legs jointed at the hips, knees and ankles, vinyl arms jointed at shoulders and elbows, sleep eyes, ash-blonde hair in elaborate original coiffure still having original hairpins and net, delicate curls at the forehead. Costume: vivid lilac tutu with satin bodice and pants, and multi-tiered ruffled net skirt, pale pink tights, pink satin ballet slippers, a coronet of pink flowers in her hair that matches the festoon of flowers on her tutu, two rhinestones at shoulder straps, solitaire ring. The costume is labeled Elise and she has her original wrist booklet and box labeled Elise 1635. Near mint, fabulous complexion with enhancing dark eye shadow, rosy cheeks, perfect coiffure and costume. Alexander, Elise Ballerina, model #1635, 1957, the costume was offered in a variety of colors as seen in this pair. $800/1100

90. Elise Ballerina in Pale Lavender Tutu, 1957

17" (43 cm.) Hard plastic socket head, adult-lady shaped body and legs with jointing at hips, knees and ankles, vinyl arms jointed at shoulders and elbows, sleep eyes, auburn hair with rolled bangs and pageboy curls still captured with original hairpins and net. Costume: pale lavender satin bodice and pants under a cloud of billowing lavender ruffed-net skirt, pink stockings, pink satin ballet slippers, a coronet of pink flowers in her hair to match the festoon of flowers on her bodice, amethyst stones dot the shoulder straps, solitaire ring. The costume is labeled Elise and she has her original wrist booklet and box labeled Elise 1635. Near mint condition, fabulous complexion, coiffure and costume. Alexander, Elise Ballerina, model 1635, 1957, identical to the preceding except hair, costume color and jewel decoration. $800/1100

91. Lissy as "Southern Belle", 1963

12" (30 cm.) All hard plastic with socket head, jointing at shoulders and hips, sleep eyes, ash-blonde hair with curly bangs and shoulder-length curls still held by original hairpins. Costume: crisp pale blue taffeta gown with ribbon and lace trim, stiffened crinoline, pantalets with three rows of lace ruffles, sock, black velvet shoes, pink sash, and woven white bonnet with wide brim lavishly trimmed with curled feathers. The costume is labeled Southern Belle, and the doll has her original wrist booklet and is presented in her original box labeled Southern Belle 1255. Near mint condition, beautiful rosy cheeks and superb coiffure and costume. Alexander, model 1255, the doll was presented as one of the Classics Group in the 1963 Alexander catalog "dressed with all the charm and grace of the south of long ago". $500/800

92. Wendy-Kins "Southern Belle", 1963

8" (20 cm.) All hard plastic with socket head, bendable-knee walking-style body, sleep eyes, ash-blonde hair with luxurious arranged curls onto shoulders. Costume: pale blue crisp taffeta dress with tiers of lace and ribbon trim, stiffened crinoline, cotton pantalets with two rows of lace edging, white socks, black velvet slip-on shoes, matching blue bonnet with lace edging and floral decoration. The costume is labeled Madame Alexander and the doll has her original wrist booklet and original box labeled Southern Belle 785. Near mint condition, beautiful rosy cheeks, perfectly preserved coiffure and costume. Alexander, 1963, a companion model to the Lissy Southern Belle. $400/600

93. Wendy-Kins "Easter", 1968 with Letter from Madame Alexander

8" (20 cm.) All hard plastic with socket head, bendable-leg walking body, sleep eyes, waist-length straight brunette hair and bangs. Costume: pale yellow polished cotton dress with lace bodice and

attached slip, white leggings, tan side-snap velvet shoes, lace-over-yellow-cotton bonnet with double row of lace ruffles around the face, tiny yellow flowers on dress and bonnet. The costume is labeled Madame Alexander, and the doll is presented in original box labeled 719. Near mint condition, bright rosy cheeks, beautiful costume and coiffure. Alexander, 1968, a photocopied letter signed by B. Alexander accompanies the doll "certifying that only 320 of the #719 dolls were produced...and were made in 1968 for the Easter Season". $400/500

94. Red-Haired Maggie Angel, 1961

8" (20 cm.) All hard plastic with socket head, bendable-knees walking-style body, green sleep eyes, freckles, impish smile, long straight red hair with bangs. Costume: aqua taffeta angel gown with gold metallic edging and yoke, silver leatherette wings, panties, silver shoes. The costume is labeled Maggie, Alexander, and she has her original Maggie Mix-up wrist booklet, and original box labeled Maggie Mix-up 618. Near mint condition, beautiful rosy cheeks, vibrant hair and crisp fresh costume and wings. Alexander, model #618, 1961, the catalog noted, presumably in Maggie's words, "if you think an angel costume is strange for Maggie Mixup, so do I, but I'm in a play about angels and that's why I have it." $400/600

95. Lissy "Bridesmaid" in Pale Lavender Ensemble, 1957

12" (30 cm.) All hard plastic with socket head, jointing at shoulders, and hips, sleep eyes, ash-blonde hair with curly bangs, waist-length hair still captured in original band and pins. Costume: pale lavender nylon gown with square-cut bodice, pouf sleeves, full-length skirt with wide band of val lace that matches bodice lace, lavender silk sash, pale pink taffeta petticoat, panties, stockings, pink sling heels, lavender tulle cloud-like bonnet tied with wide tulle streamers, carrying a nosegay of tiny flowers, pearl tear-drop earrings. The costume is labeled Lissy, Madame Alexander, and the doll is presented in her original box with FAO Schwarz label. Near mint condition, beautifully preserved costume and fabulous original hair arrangement. Alexander, model 1161, the model was described in the 1957 catalog as "beautiful bridesmaid". $600/800

96. "Kathy" in Peach Organdy Dress and Lace Bonnet, 1958

11" (28 cm.) All vinyl doll with socket head, five piece body. large blue sleep eyes, blonde rooted hair, mouth with baby bottle hole. Costume: peach organdy baby dress with lace trim, matching bonnet with three rows of ruffles and pink bows, pink taffeta slip and panties, socks, lace-trimmed shoes with pink bows, with pacifier. The doll is presented in near mint condition in its original box labeled "Kathy", model 2710. Alexander, circa 1958. $200/300

96.1. "Littlest Kitten" in Pale Pink Organdy Dress, 1960

8" (20 cm.) All-vinyl doll with socket head and five-piece body, blonde rooted short baby hair in delicate tendrils, blue eyes. Costume: palest pink organdy dress with generous lace edging and pearl buttons that extend down the back, matching petticoat and panties, pink socks with petal trim, holding a baby bottle. The doll is preserved in near mint unplayed with condition in its original box labeled "Littlest Kitten", model 540. Alexander, the model was shown in the company's 1960 catalog. $200/300

97. Little Genius in Coat and Bonnet, 1956

8" (20 cm.) Hard plastic socket head, rigid vinyl five piece baby body, dark sleep eyes, mouth sculpted for baby bottle, blonde fleeced wig. Costume: full-length organdy baby gown with lace trim, satin petticoat and lace-edged diaper, white gabardine full-length coat with satin lining, matching bonnet with white satin ribbons, with baby bottle. The costume is labeled Madame Alexander, and the doll is presented in original box labeled 780 with original FAO Schwarz store label. Near mint condition, beautiful complexion and costume. Alexander, Little Genius, model 780, presented in 1956. $300/500

98. Little Genius "Nothing Could be Finer", 1957

8" (20 cm.) Hard plastic socket head, rigid vinyl five piece baby body, mouth sculpted for baby bottle, blonde flocked hair. Costume: white organdy baby dress with lace-edged Bertha collar to match lace at hem and bonnet ruffled;

the dress with applique floral design on collar, lace-edged petticoat and diaper, pink socks with floral decorations, with original baby bottle. The costume is labeled Madame Alexander and the doll has her original wrist booklet and box labled Little Genius 246. Near mint condition, beautiful complexion and costume. Alexander, model #246, described in the 1957 catalog as "nothing could be finer... expecting to be the center of attention when the Aunts and Uncles come to call." $300/500

99. Little Genius "Ready for Her First Party", Blue Accents, 1956

8" (20 cm.) Hard plastic socket head, rigid vinyl five piece baby body, blonde flocked hair, sleep eyes, mouth sculpted for bottle. Costume: white organdy baby dress with blue sash and

embroidery, lace-edged bonnet with blue ribbons, petticoat, lace-edged flannel diaper, socks with blue floral medallions. The costume is labeled Madame Alexander, the doll has original wrist booklet, and is presented in original box labeled 742 Blue. Near mint, beautiful rosy cheeks, softest hair, fresh costume. Alexander, Little Genius model #742 described in the 1956 catalog as "all ready for her first little party". $300/500

100. Little Genius "Ready for Her First Party", Pink Accents", 1956

8" (20 cm.) Hard plastic socket head, five piece rigid vinyl baby body, sleep eyes, flocked blonde hair. Costume: pink organdy baby dress with embroidered pink flowers on the bodice, feather-stitching around the skirt and lace trim, with matching bonnet having beautiful floral embroidery on the sides, pink cotton petticoat, lace-edged pink diaper, socks with pink floral medallions, with baby bottle. The costume is labeled Madame Alexander and the doll has its original wrist booklet and is presented in original box labeled 742 Pink. Near mint condition, perfectly preserved. Alexander, model 742, the doll was described as "ready for her first party" in the firm's 1956 catalog. $300/500

101. Wendy-Kins Nurse and Baby in Striped Uniform, 1964

8" (20 cm.) All hard plastic with socket head, bendable-knees walking-style body, sleep eyes, bright blonde hair with curly bangs and flip curls. Costume: blue and white striped nurse's uniform with white bib apron and nurse's cap, panties, socks, laced shoes, carrying little celluloid baby with cut-work cotton gown. The costume is labeled Wendy-Kins and the doll is presented with her original wrist tag and in original Alexander box labeled Wendy-Kins 660. Near mint condition, bright rosy cheeks, fresh and crisp costume and coiffure. Alexander, model 660, 1964. $400/600

102. Basic Wendy, 1956

8" (20 cm.) All hard plastic with socket head, bendable-knees walking-style body, sleep eyes, brunette hair with bangs and flip curls. Costume: pink taffeta panties with lace edgings, white socks, black velvet side-snap shoes.

The pants are labeled Alexander-kins and the doll is presented in her original box labeled 500, along with a photograph of Madame Alexander, a 1956 Little People catalog, and a brochure for Start-A-Home for Alexander-kins furniture. Near mint condition. Alexander, model #500, 1956. $200/400

103. Basic Little Genius, 1957

8" (20 cm.) Hard plastic socket head, rigid plastic five piece baby body, blonde flocked hair, sleep eyes, mouth sculpted for baby bottle. Costume: peach dotted Swiss panties with lace trim, socks, pink floral medallions, with baby bottle. The costume is labeled Little Genius and the doll has original wrist booklet and box labeled Little Genius 200. Near mint condition of the doll and existing costume; according to original catalog description the costume included a top and bonnet. Alexander, 1957. $200/300

105. Wendy-Kins Bride "What Could be Sweeter?", 1961

8" (20 cm.) All hard plastic with socket head, bendable-knee walking-style body, sleep eyes, brunette hair with curly bangs and flip curls. Costume: white tulle gown with applique floral-tatted borders and bead edging at the neckline, pouf sleeves, organdy petticoat, panties, garter, pale golden satin shoes, an exuberant coronet of flowers with tulle veil and matching bridal bouquet. The costume is labeled Alexander-Kins and she has her original wrist booklet and box labeled Wendy-Kins 480. Near mint condition, perfectly preserved costume, coiffure and rosy cheeks. Alexander, model 480, 1961 described as "what could be sweeter...enveloped in a mist of white tulle.". $300/500

106. Red-haired Wendy-Kins Bride, 1963

8" (20 cm.) All hard plastic with socket head, bendable knee walking-style body, sleep eyes, auburn hair with curly bangs and flip curls. Costume: white nylon tulle long-sleeved gown with three rows of lace at the hem and two on the bodice, white sash, organdy petticoat, panties, garter, pale golden slipper shoes, very extravagant coronet of delicate flowers that matches her bridal bouquet. The costume is labeled Wendy-Kins and she has her original wrist booklet and original box labeled Wendy-Kins 470. Near mint condition, gorgeous face and hair, very beautiful and highly detailed costume and accessories. Alexander, model 470, 1963. $300/500

104. Alexander-Kins Bridesgroom, 1958

8" (20 cm.) All hard plastic with socket head, bendable-knee walking-style body, brunette side-parted flocked hair with stylish wave at the forehead, sleep eyes. Costume: black velvet formal jacket with tails and silk lapels, floral boutonniere, shirt, grey silk tie with faux-diamond stickpin, cummerbund, striped trousers, black socks, black side-snap shoes. The costume is labeled Alexander-kins and he is presented in his original box labeled 572. Near mint condition. rosy cheeks, perfect coiffure and costume. Alexander, model #572, the doll appeared in the 1958 catalog described as "dressed impeccably" yet in typical Bridegroom manner "looks a bit bewildered". $400/600

107. Wendy-Kins Bride, 1966

8" (20 cm.) All hard plastic with socket head, bendable-knee walking-style body, dark brunette hair with curly bangs and flip curls, sleep eyes. Costume: white tulle gown with Juliet sleeves and lace trim, tulle and organdy petticoats, taffeta panties, garter, gold shoes, coronet

of white lilies with lace-edged tulle veil, matching bridal bouquet. The costume is labeled Madame Alexander and she has an original wrist booklet and box labeled Bride 735. Near mint, beautiful complexion, coiffure, wonderful costume. Alexander, model 735. 1966. $300/400

108. Cissette "Southern Belle" Portrette in Window Box, 1968

10" (25 cm.) All hard plastic with socket head, adult lady-shaped body, jointing at shoulders, hips and knees, high-heel shaped feet, sleep eyes, bright blonde hair with curly bangs and flip curls. Costume: white nylon full-length gown with multi-tiered skirt, green silk ribbon and lace trim, nylon underskirt, taffeta can-can petticoat,, panties, stockings,

green heeled shoes, large white bonnet with over-sized roses. The costume is labeled Southern Belle, and the doll has her original wrist booklet and maroon/gold window box. Near mint condition, box wear. Alexander, model #1170, from the 1968 Portrette Series. $300/500

109. Cissette "Scarlett" Portrette in Window Box, 1968

10" (25 cm.) All hard plastic with socket head, adult lady-shaped body with jointing at shoulders, hips and knees, high-heel shaped feet, sleep eyes, dark brunette hair with long flowing curls onto shoulders. Costume: emerald green taffeta gown with black soutache trim, removable matching jacket, taffeta can-can petticoat, panties, stockings, black heeled shoes, green taffeta bonnet with pink floral trim. The costume is labeled Scarlett and the doll has her original wrist booklet and is presented in her original window box. Near mint condition. Alexander, model #1174, from the 1968 Portrette Series. $300/500

110. Wendy-Kins "Scarlett O'Hara", 1965

8" (20 cm.) All hard plastic with socket head, bendable-knee walking-style body, sleep eyes, brunette hair with curly bangs and rolled curls. Costume: crispy cream taffeta gown with hem ruffle and green rick-rack trim, green silk sash, pink rosebud trim, cotton petticoat and pantalets with lace edging, white socks, black velvet slippers, woven bonnet with wide brim decorated with green brim and three rosebuds and leaves. The costume is labeled Scarlett O'Hara and the doll has her original wrist booklet and is preserved in her original box labeled Scarlett O'Hara 785. Near mint condition, superb preservation of costume and coiffure, lovely complexion. Alexander, model #785, 1965. $400/600

111. Set, Lissy Dolls as "Little Women", 1962

12" (30 cm.) All hard plastic with socket head, jointing at shoulders and hips, sleep eyes, and each with unique hair color and style to define the personality of the storybook character. Costumes: each wears her original cotton or taffeta costume with accessories and shoes. Each costume is labeled with the name of the doll (Marme, Meg, Jo, Beth or Amy) and Little Women, Madame Alexander. Near mint, beautifully preserved costumes and coiffure, lovely complexions. Alexander, from the #1225 series of Little Women, presented in the 1962 catalog. $800/1200

112. Lissy as Cinderella Gift Set, 1966, from FAO Schwarz

12" (30 cm.) All hard plastic with socket head, jointing at shoulders and hips, sleep eyes, ash-blonde hair with curly bangs, side hair drawn back into cluster of curls at the back crown and falling onto her shoulders. Costume: aqua satin gown with rows of ruffled lace in a matching color around the neckline, sleeves and skirt, silver metallic appliques and rose buds, aqua taffeta can-can petticoat, aqua taffeta panties with lace trim, stockings, flat silver shoes and "glittering tiara" with eight large faux-diamonds. Also included is "scullery maid" costume comprising green cotton dress and orange apron with felt patches, green scarf, brown felt shoes, socks, cotton panties, and broom. The costume is labeled Cinderella, and the doll has her wrist booklet and is preserved in her original window gift box. Near mint, gorgeous costume, coiffure and complexion. Alexander, model 1240, 1966, the terms "glittering tiara" and "scullery maid" were used in the catalog description of that year; the box has original FAO Schwarz store label $600/900

113. Lissy as McGuffey Ana, 1963

12" (30 cm.) All hard plastic, socket head, jointing at shoulders and hips, dark sleep eyes, ash-blonde hair with rolled bangs and waist-length braids tied with red silk ribbons. Costume: red velvet winter ensemble, the dress featuring a white satin faille bodice and widely flared red velvet skirt with white satin lining that has an attached tulle ruffle, matching long-sleeved red velvet fully-lined jacket with self-covered buttons and white plush collar, matching white plush mittens and cap with red pom-pom, knit white leggings, black shoes with red felt spats. The costume is labeled Madame Alexander, and the doll has her original wrist booklet and is preserved in her original box labeled McGuffey Ana 1258. Near mint condition, gorgeous cheek coloring and coiffure with little curls at braid tips, vibrant fresh costume. Alexander, model #1258, 1963. $600/900

114. Lissy as "Katie" 100th Anniversary Doll for FAO Schwarz, 1962

12" (30 cm.) All hard plastic, socket head, jointing at shoulders and hips, green sleep eyes, brunette hair arranged with deep curls onto her forehead and tumbling onto her shoulders. Costume: yellow taffeta gown with lace edging and russet velvet sash, white cotton petticoat and pantalets trimmed with lace and yellow silk ribbons, white knit stockings, light brown suede-like slippers, cotton Charlotte bonnet with lace edging and russet velvet band. The costume is labeled Madame Alexander, and the doll has her original wrist booklet and original box labeled 1241. Near mint condition, gorgeous coiffure, fresh and vibrant complexion and costume. Alexander, model 1241, 1962, the doll was produced exclusively for FAO Schwarz 100th anniversary and has original store label and additional store silver bell label "Est. 1862 Toys FAO Schwarz, 100 Years in Toys". $500/800

115. Lissy as "Tommy", 100th Anniversary Doll for FAO Schwarz, 1962

12" (30 cm.) Hard plastic socket head, jointing at shoulders and hips, sleep eyes, blonde hair in side-part and short boyish fashion. Costume: aqua cotton gabardine suit with tiny pearl buttons, white Peter Pan collar, striped knit stockings, tan suede like shoes, straw bowler with black streamer. The costume is labeled Madame Alexander and the doll has its original wrist booklet and is preserved in its original box labeled 1240. Near mint, beautifully preserved complexion, coiffure and costume. Alexander, model 1240, 1962, the doll was created as a companion doll for Katie for the 100th anniversary of FAO Schwarz; the box has two original FAO Schwarz labels including silver bell label. $500/800

116. Basic Cissette, First Year Model 1957

10" (25 cm.) All hard plastic, socket head, adult lady-shaped body, jointing at shoulders, hips and knees, high-heel shaped feet, sleep eyes, bright blonde hair with curly bangs, mid-back length curls captured in original cluster with pink silk ribbon at nape. Costume: earliest model lace chemise with pink bow and rose, stockings, pink sling heels with rhinestones. The costume is labeled Cissette, and the doll is presented in her original box labeled 900B Blonde. Near mint, perfectly preserved coiffure and costume, lovely complexion. Alexander, Basic Cissette, the first model of the lingerie-attired Cissette, model 900B, 1957. $300/500

117. Cissette Beauty Queen with Trophy. c. 1959

10" (25 cm.) All hard plastic with socket head, adult lady-shaped body with jointing at shoulders, hips, and knees, high-heel shaped feet, sleep eyes, ash-blonde hair with curly bangs and flip curls. Costume: blue taffeta swim suit with silver trim at edges, yellow silk banner with brass eagle emblem and blue ribbon away, stockings, sling heels with blue floral medallion, and carrying a trophy award. The costume is labeled Cissette and the doll is presented with original wrist booklet in box labeled Cissette 700. Near mint condition. Alexander, circa. 1959. $400/600

118. Cissette "Attending Tea", 1957

10" (25 cm.) All hard plastic, socket head, jointing at shoulder, elbows and knees, high-heel shaped feet, sleep eyes, brunette hair with original short forehead bangs, and arranged rolled curls. Costume: aqua taffeta faille afternoon dress with fitted bodice, pink taffeta petticoat and panties with lace edging, stockings, pink sling heels, pearls, stiffened-lace bonnet with interwoven rose ribbons and rose-tinged floral cluster that matches the "modest corsage" (1957 catalog description) at her waist. The costume is labeled Cissette and the doll is presented in her original box labeled 918. Near mint condition, crisp and fresh throughout. Alexander, model 918, the doll appeared in the 1957 catalog described as "smart from head to hem". $500/800

119. Cissette in Stylish "Outfits for Every Occasion" Ensemble, 1958

10" (25 cm.) All hard plastic with socket head, adult female-shaped torso, jointing at shoulders, hips and knees, high-heel shaped feet. Costume: black knit sweater, gold-patterned red cotton box-pleated skirt with wide gold belt, scalloped-edge net petticoat with interwoven design, taffeta lace-edged panties, stockings, gold sling heels, necklace chain, pearl drop earrings, woven bonnet with black velvet band and bow. The costume is labeled Cissette and the doll is presented in her original box labeled 815. Near mint condition with perfectly kept coiffure, vibrant costume, rosy cheeks. Alexander, model 815, the doll appeared in the 1958 catalog indicating that Cissette had "outfits for every occasion"; an identical matching costume was made for Cissy that same year. $500/800

120. Cissette Wears "Sheer Cotton for a Sunny Day", 1958

10" (25 cm.) All hard plastic, socket head, adult female-shaped torso, jointing at shoulders, hips and knees, high-heel shaped feet, sleep eyes, brunette hair with curly bangs and flip curls. Costume: airy cotton dress of tiny lavender and white checkered design with lace edging peeking out at hem of skirt and forming sleevelets, lace-edged petticoat and panties, stockings, white/silver sling heels, woven lavender bonnet generously decorated with tulle, lavender velvet ribbon and lilacs and little bluettes that are repeated at her waist. The costume is labeled Cissette and she is presented in her original box labeled Cissette 821. Near mint, beautiful complexion and coiffure, very fresh and vibrant costume. Alexander, model #821, the doll appeared in the 1958 catalog, her hat described as "frames her face with charm". $500/800

121. Cissette "Likes Smart Cotton Frocks", 1959

10" (25 cm.) All hard plastic with socket head, adult lady-shaped torso, jointing at shoulders, hips and knees, high-heel shaped feet, sleep eyes, ash-blonde hair with curly bangs and flip curls. Costume: polka dot dress of polished cotton with wide lace-edged Bertha collar extended pink velvet ribbons, lace-edged taffeta petticoat and panties, stockings, black sling heels, pearl earrings, and white woven bonnet with extravagant brim of bright pink roses and little white flowers. The dress is labeled Cissette, and the doll has her original wrist booklet and is preserved in original box labeled Cissette 722. Near mint condition, gorgeous rosy-cheeked complexion, beautiful coiffure, fresh and vibrant costume. Alexander, model #722, the doll appeared in the firm's 1959 catalog. $500/800

120.

119.

121.

122. Cissy in "Never Looked Prettier" Navy Blue Taffeta, 1955

20" (51 cm.) Hard plastic socket head, adult lady-shaped torso and legs with jointing at hips and knees and high-heel shaped feet, vinyl arms jointed at shoulders and elbows, sleep eyes, ash-blonde hair with curly bangs and generous curls at sides and back of head. Costume: navy blue taffeta afternoon dress with black braid trim and navy blue tulle sleevelets, matching bolero jacket with white faille bow, taffeta can-can petticoat with rick-rack trim, lace-edged panties, stockings, black sling heels, sky-blue woven bonnet with wide brim edged in lace and a garland of berries and leaves. The costume is labeled Cissy, the doll has her original wrist booklet, and she is preserved in her original box labeled Cissy 2084. Near mint condition, beautiful complexion, crisp and fresh costume. Alexander, model #2084, the doll appeared in the premiere year of Cissy, 1955, described as "Cissy never looked prettier".
$900/1200

123. Cissy "Looks so Charming", 1956

20" (51 cm.) Hard plastic socket head, adult lady-shaped torso and legs jointed at hips and knees, high-heel shaped feet, vinyl arms with shoulder and elbow jointing, sleep eyes, ash-blonde hair with curly bangs and arranged shoulder-length hair. Costume: aqua taffeta cocktail dress with shaped bodice and dropped waist above very full skirt, removable black velvet bolero with pink rose corsage, pink taffeta can-can petticoat and panties, stockings, silver sling heels, rhinestone bracelet, and a black velvet wide head band with attached facial veil and lavish floral decorations. The costume is labeled Cissy and the doll is presented in her original box labeled 2017. Near mint condition, beautiful complexion, coiffure and costume. Alexander, model #2017, the doll appeared in the 1956 catalog described as looking "so charming in a smart cock dress". $800/1200

124. Basic Cissette, 1962 Model

10" (25 cm.) All hard plastic with socket head, adult lady-shaped torso, jointing at shoulders, hips and knees, sleep eyes, light blonde hair with curly bangs and flip curls. Costume: lacy chemise, stockings, gold sling heels, pearl earrings. The costume is tagged Cissette and the doll has her original wrist booklet and is preserved in her original box labeled Cissette 700. Near mint, gorgeous complexion and coiffure. Alexander, the second model of Basic Cissette with variation in hair style and chemise from the 1957 original, model #700. 1962, the doll was described in the catalog as a "beautiful debutante doll...the color of rare porcelaine". $400/600

125. Jacqueline in Blue Suit, 1962

10" (25 cm.) All hard plastic with socket head, adult lady-shaped torso, jointing at shoulders, hips and knees. high-heel shaped feet, sleep eyes, blue eye shadow, brunette hair in side-part with side spit curl, rolled curls. Costume: two piece blue boucle suit with satin lining, self-covered buttons, cropped jacket, matching pillbox style hat, panties, stockings, black sling heels, pearl earrings. The costume is labeled Jacqueline, and the doll has original wrist booklet and is in her original box labeled Jacqueline 894. Near mint condition. Alexander, model #894, 1962. $400/600

126. Margot "New and Beautiful" in Bikini, 1961

10" (25 cm.) All hard plastic, socket head, adult lady-shaped torso, jointing at shoulders, knees and hips, high-heel shaped feet, sleep eyes, blue eye shadow, brunette hair in elaborate arrangement. Costume: two piece bikini swim suit, black sling heels, pearl drop earrings. The costume is labeled

Margot, and she has her original wrist booklet and original box labeled Margot 900. Near mint condition, very beautiful complexion and coiffure, Alexander, model 900 Margot was newly presented in 1961 described as "new and beautiful" with her "hairdo upswept and high high on her hand". $500/800

127. Cissette in Blue Sun-Bathing Suit, 1961

10" (25 cm.) All hard plastic, socket head, adult lady-shaped torso, jointing at shoulders, hips and knees, high-heel shaped feet, sleep eyes, blonde hair with curly bangs and flip curls. Costume: royal blue taffeta sun-bathing suit with silver and braid trim, pearl drop earrings, white sling strap heels. The costume is labeled Cissette, and the doll has her original wrist booklet and box labeled Cissette 800. Near mint condition, fabulous cheek color and coiffure, vibrant and fresh costume. Alexander, model 800, 1961. $500/700

128. Margot "Looks Especially Chic", 1961

10" (25 cm.) All hard plastic with socket head, adult lady-shaped torso, jointing at shoulders, hips and knees, high-heel shaped feet, sleep eyes, blue eye shadow, bright blonde hair in elaborate

upswept fashion with side spit curl at the forehead. Costume: blue satin sheath with detachable faux-lambswool stole, panties, stockings, black sling shoes, pearls, faux-diamond earrings. The costume is labeled Margot and she has her original wrist booklet and box labeled Margot 910. Near mint condition, perfectly preserved coiffure, costume and beautiful complexion. Alexander, model #901, the doll appeared in the 1961 catalog described as looking "especially chic...in satin gown for afternoon wear". $500/800

129. Margot in Lilac Satin Evening Gown, 1961

10" (25 cm.) All hard plastic with socket head, adult lacy-shaped torso, jointing at shoulder, hips and knees, high-heel shaped feet, sleep eyes, blue eye shadow, blonde hair arranged in an elaborate upswept fashion with spit curl onto forehead and lilac velvet hair bow. Costume: rich lilac satin evening gown with flared shape, decorated with a band of lilac sequins, pink taffeta can-can petticoat, lace-edged panties, stockings, gold sling heels, three-faux-diamond dangle earrings with prism cut that captures the color of the gown. The costume is labeled Margot and the doll has her original wrist booklet and is in her original box labeled Margot 920. Near mint condition, fabulous complexion, coiffure and costume. Alexander, model #920, the costume was described in the Alexander 1961 catalog as "the color of French lilacs", and the box has its original FAO Schwarz store label. $500/800

130. Wendy-Kins Ballerina in Yellow Sequin Tutu, 1965

8" (20 cm.) All hard plastic with socket head, bendable-knees walking style body, sleep eyes, blonde hair with curly bangs, hair swept back into curls at the crown decorated with tiny flowers, curls all around the sides and back. Costume: yellow tulle and satin tutu with yellow sequins on the bodice, attached panties with yellow tutu ruffles, yellow satin shoes with yellow bows. The costume is labeled Wendy-kins, ant the doll is presented with original wrist booklet in her box labeled 620. Near mint condition, beautiful costume, bright rosy cheeks, perfect coiffure. Alexander, model #620, 1965. $300/400

131. Wendy "Loves Ballet Lessons", 1956

8" (20 cm.) All hard plastic with socket head, bendable-knees walking style body, sleep eyes, brunette hair with curly bangs and shoulder-length curls. Costume: magenta tulle and satin faille tutu with layers of ruffles, tiny white lilies of the valley in hair and at waist, peach satin shoes with pink ties. The costume is labeled Alexander-Kins, and the doll is presented in her original box labeled 564. Near mint condition. Alexander, model #564, 1956, the doll was described in that year's catalog as "Wendy loves ballet lessons". $400/600

132. Wendy-Kins in White Ballerina Tutu, 1966

All hard plastic, socket head, bendable-knee non-walking-style body, sleep eyes, brunette hair with curly bangs, cluster of curls and flowers at the crown, soft curls all around. Costume: white satin and tulle tutu with white sequin trim at the waist, and applique flowers with rhinestone centers scattered on bodice and skirt, peach satin shoes with pink ties. The costume is labeled Madame Alexander, and the doll is presented with original wrist booklet in original box, labeled 730. Near mint condition. Alexander, 1966. $200/300

133. Wendy-Kins in Blue Ballerina Tutu, 1966

8" (20 cm.) All hard plastic, socket head, bendable-knee non-walking body, sleep eyes, brunette hair with curly bangs, cluster of curls and flowers at the crown, curls overall. Costume: blue satin and tulle tutu with sequin detailed waist, and applique flowers with rhinestone centers, peach slippers with pink bows. The costume is labeled Madame Alexander, and the doll is presented in her original box labeled 730. Near mint condition. Alexander, model 730, 1966. $200/300

134. Maggie Mix-Up in Green Slacks, 1961

8" (20 cm.) All hard plastic, socket head, bendable-knee walking style body, freckles, green sleep eyes, straight red hair with bangs. Costume, white knit shirt and cap, green cotton slacks with gold elastic waist band, sandals. The costume is labeled Maggie Mixup and the doll has her original wrist booklet and box labeled 595. Near mint condition, wonderful complexion and vibrant costume and hair. Alexander, model 595, 1961. $300/500

135. Maggie Mixup in "Favorite School Dress", 1961

8" (20 cm.) All hard plastic, socket head, bendable-knee walking-style body, green sleep eyes, freckles, straight red hair and bangs. Costume: blue and white cotton checkered

134, 135.

print dress with wide sash and matching pantalets trimmed with lace, Peter Pan collar, white socks, tan side-snap shoes, white woven hat with blue bows. The costume is tagged Maggie Mixup and the doll is presented in her original box labeled Maggie Mixup 617. Near mint condition, beautiful hair, complexion and costume. Alexander, model #617, 1961, the costume was described in that year's catalog as Maggie's "favorite school dress", and the box has original store label of FAO Schwarz. $400/600

136. Maggie Mixup in Blue Slacks, 1960

16" (41 cm.) Hard plastic socket head, adult lady-shaped torso and legs jointed at hips and knees, vinyl arms with jointing at elbows and shoulders. green sleep eyes, freckles, long straight red hair with bangs. Costume: white knit shirt, blue cotton pleated slacks, colorful sash, blue leatherette shoes with impressed star design, chain necklace with blue stone, woven hat with colorful band to match her sash. The costume is labeled Maggie Mixup and the doll has her original wrist booklet and is presented in her original box labeled Maggie Mixup 1811. Near mint condition, vibrant colors of complexion, hair and costume. Alexander, model #1811, 1960. $500/800

137. Cissette as "Gibson Girl" in Purple Velvet, 1962

10" (25 cm.) All hard plastic with socket head, adult lady-torso, jointed arms and legs with bendable knees, high-heel feet, brunette hair with side-swept bangs and side spit curl, chignon, sleep eyes. Costume: lavender and white striped cotton blouse with purple bow, vivid purple velvet long skirt, faux leather belt, lavender straw bonnet with lavish feathered and black tulle, white taffeta petticoat, panties, stockings, black sling heels, rhinestone earrings and solitaire. The costume is tagged Madame Alexander, the doll has original gold wrist tag "Gibson Girl" along with a brochure advertising Miss Melinda who writes letters, and is in her original box stamped "Gibson Girl 760". Near mint condition, gorgeous complexion and coiffure, extravagant and fresh costume. Alexander, model 760, "Gibson Girl", 1962. $400/600

138. Cissette as "Gibson Girl" in Rose-Flowered Bonnet, 1963

10" (25 cm.) All hard plastic with socket head, adult-lady shaped torso, jointing at shoulders and hips, bendable knees, brunette hair arranged in neatly coiffed chignon with side spit curl at forehead, sleep eyes. Costume: white organdy shirtwaist blouse with lace trim, black velvet long skirt, taffeta petticoat, panties, stockings, black sling heels, woven bonnet with five roses arranged at the front of the brim, rhinestone earrings and belt buckle. The costume is labeled "Cissette", the doll has her original gold wrist tag "Gibson Girl" and she is presented in her original box labeled "Gibson Girl 760". Near mint unplayed with condition. Alexander, model 760 of 1963. $400/500

139. Cissette as "Melanie" in Yellow Ruffled Lace Ball Gown, 1968

10" (25 cm.) All hard plastic with socket head, adult-lady shaped torso, jointing at shoulder and hips, bendable knees, high-heel shaped feet, sleep eyes, golden blonde hair with long arranged curls onto her shoulders and long bangs drawn back to ribboned curls at each side of face. Costume: yellow organdy gown with eight rows of ruffled matched lace on the skirt, attached frou-frou petticoat, panties, stockings, gold sling heels, yellow sash with floral appliques that are repeated on the skirt. The costume is labeled "Melanie", The doll is in her original box labeled "Melanie 1182"

in pristine near mint condition with fresh vibrant colors of costume, cheeks and coiffure. Alexander Melanie, 1968. $300/500

140. "Cissette" Ballerina in Pink Tutu with White Floral Coronet, 1963

10" (25 cm.) All hard plastic with socket head, adult-lady shaped torso, jointing at shoulders and hips, bendable knees, high-heel posed feet, sleep eyes, brunette hair with bangs and captured curls at the nape. Costume: pink tulle and satin tutu with rhinestone trim, pink satin sash, pale pink stockings, ballet-slippers, and having a lavish coronet of white flowers with centered pink rose, white flowers at her shoulders, rhinestone earrings. The costume is tagged Cissette, and the doll has her original wrist booklet and original box labeled Cissette 735. Near mint condition, beautifully blushed cheeks, perfect coiffure and costume. Alexander, 1963. $300/500

141. "Cissette" Ballerina in Pink Tutu and Pink Floral Coronet, 1963

10" (25 cm.) A slight variation of #140, having duplicate costume, coiffure and accessories, except the coronet and shoulder corsages are comprised of pink-petal pink flowers with tiny yellow centers, The costume is tagged Cissette and the doll has her original wrist booklet and original box labeled Cissette 735. Near mint condition, beautiful complexion, coiffure and costume. Alexander, 1963. $300/500

142. "Cissette" Ballerina in Pink Tutu with Tiny Petal Garlands, 1962

10" (25 cm.) All hard plastic with swivel head, adult-lady shaped torso, jointing at shoulders and hips, bendable knees, high-heel posed feet, brunette coiffure with curled bangs and cluster of curls at the nape, sleep eyes. Costume: pink tulle and satin tutu, satin panties, stockings, ballet slippers, rhinestone earrings, corsages of tiny pink and white lilies of the valley at the side of hair and at her waist. Excellent condition. She wears her original wrist booklet and is preserved in her original box labeled Cissette 737. Alexander, circa 1962. $300/400

143. "Cissette" in Black and White Checkered Suit, 1963

10" (25 cm.) All hard plastic with socket head, adult-lady shaped torso, jointing at shoulder and hips, bendable knees, high-heel posed feet, brunette bouffant hair style, sleep eyes. Costume: black and white checkered suit with cropped jacket, white collar, black buttons and bow, sheath skirt, panties, stockings, black sling heels, pearl drop earrings, solitaire, white woven hat with grosgrain band. The costume is tagged "Cissette" and the doll has her original wrist booklet and is in non-original Alexander box. Near mint condition of doll, beautiful fresh costume and complexion, perfectly kept coiffure. Alexander, model 746, the doll was offered in the 1963 Alexander catalog. $400/600

144. Elise Ballerina with Kelly Face in Pink Tutu, Circa 1963

17". Hard plastic socket head with facial model used for Kelly doll, standard Elise body with jointing at shoulders, elbows, hips, knees and ankles, blonde hair with original elaborate coiffure and floral coronet. Costume: pink satin and tulle tutu with pink sash and floral appliques, stockings, peach ballerina shoes, faux-diamond earrings. The costume is labeled Elise and the doll has her original wrist booklet and box labeled Elise 15-232. Near mint condition. Alexander, circa 1963, the head is completely original to the Elise Ballerina, and has original and matching coiffure to costume. $500/800

145. "Elise" Ballerina in Pink Tutu with Coronet of Roses, 1964

16" (46 cm.) Vinyl socket head, adult-lady modeled hard plastic torso and legs with jointing at hips, knees and ankles, rigid vinyl arms with jointing at shoulders and elbows, sleep eyes, golden blonde hair with bangs and uniquely arranged chignon at her nape. Costume: pink nylon tulle and satin tutu with satin sash and panties, stockings, ballet slippers, coronet of three large roses and leaves, floral sprigs on costume, rhinestone earrings The costume is tagged "Elise" and the doll has her original wrist booklet and is presented in her original box labeled Elise 1720. Near mint condition, gorgeous coiffure, beautiful complexion and costume accessories. Alexander 1964, the doll appeared in the company catalog of that year with lavish description. $300/500

146. "Elise" in Blue Ball Gown

16" (41 cm.) Vinyl socket head, hard plastic adult-lady shaped torso and legs with bendable knees and ankles, rigid vinyl arms with jointing at shoulders and elbows, sleep eyes, brunette hair with curly bangs, chignon at crown and captured curls at the nape. Costume: pale blue organdy ball gown with three tiers of ruffles at the bodice above 18 tiers of lace ruffles on the skirt, blue taffeta frou-frou petticoat, panties, stockings, silver sling heels, flowers in hair and accents on gown, pearl necklace and earrings, solitaire, elbow-length gloves. The costume is labeled Elise and the doll has her original wrist booklet and is presented in her original box labeled Elise 1735. near mint condition. Alexander, 1964. $500/700

147. "Elise" Bride in Multi-Tiered Lace Wedding Gown, 1964

16" (46 cm.) Vinyl socket head, hard plastic adult-lady shaped torso and legs with jointing at hips, knees and ankles, rigid vinyl arms with shoulder and elbow jointing, sleep eyes, brunette hair with waved bangs and luxurious flip curls. Costume: white sheer nylon gown with lace bodice and cap sleeves, five tiers of ruffled lace on the skirt, ivory sash and bow, frou-frou taffeta petticoat, panties, stockings, silver sling heels, coronet of white roses with tulle chapel length veil, lavish bouquet of flowers, pearl necklace and earrings, rhinestone ring. Her costume is tagged Elise and she has her original wrist booklet and original box labeled Elise 1740. Excellent unplayed with condition, beautifully preserved lavish costume. Alexander, 1964, the doll appeared in the the Alexander catalog of that year with the notation "everybody loves a bride and who could help loving this doll". $600/900

148. "Jacqueline" in White Satin Ball Gown and Matching Coat, 1961

21" (53 cm.) Vinyl socket head, hard plastic adult-shaped lady torso and legs with jointing at hips and knees, high-heel posed feet, rigid vinyl arms with shoulder and elbow jointing, brown sleep eyes, brunette bouffant coiffure with side part. Costume: rich white satin strapless gown decorated with bands of soutache braid accented with tiny silver beads, matching full-length coat with stand-up collar and silver floral clasp, frou-frou petticoant, panties, stockings, silver sling heels, floral-shaped silver earrings set with three pearls, double-band rhinestone bracelet, large "diamond:" ring, pearl handbag. The doll has her original wrist booklet "Jacqueline" and is presented in her original box labeled Jacqueline 2210. Alexander, the doll was presented in the 1961 catalog described as having "long curling lashes which sparkle as brightly as her jewels". $700/900

149. "Melanie Coco" in Blue Taffeta Gown, 1966

21" (53 cm.) Vinyl socket head with unique modeling used for this 1966 portrait series only, hard plastic adult-lady shaped torso with unique swivel waist, jointing at hips, legs uniquely shaped in model-like pose, sleep eyes, blonde rooted hair in very elaborate coiffure with wispy bangs and decorative flowers. Costume: blue taffeta gown in classic style with narrow pleats at the front edged by borders of lace, taffeta frou-frou petticoat, panties, stockings, satin

shoes, cameo necklace, large "diamond" ring. The costume is labeled Alexander, and the doll has her original wrist booklet and is presented in original box labeled Melanie 2050. Near mint condition, pristine costume and coiffure, very beautiful complexion. Alexander, 1966, the model was presented for one year only. $900/1400

panties, stockings, pink sling heels, black velvet bonnet with rose satin streamers and silk roses, "diamond" ring. The costume is tagged Godey, the doll has her original wrist booklet and is preserved in her original box labeled Godey 2161. Near mint condition. Alexander, the doll appeared in the 1971 catalog which, that year, offered only four models from the portrait series; few examples were made. $300/600

151. "Jenny Lind" Portrait Series, 1969

21" (53 cm.) Vinyl socket head, adult-shaped lady body, sleep eyes, blonde hair with center part arranged with intricate loop curls at the sides and decorated with pink rosebuds at each side. Costume: rose satin gown with wide panniers and lace trim, taffeta frou-frou petticoat, pantalets, pink sling heels, elaborate "diamond" earrings, solitaire, bouquet of sweetheart roses. The costume is labeled Jenny Lind, the doll has her original wrist booklet and is presented in her original box labeled Jenny Lind, 2191. Near mint condition. Alexander, the model was made for one year only in 1969. $400/700

152. "Jenny Lind" from Classics Series, Circa 1969

14" (36 cm.) Vinyl socket head, rigid plastic body, sleep eyes, blonde hair with center-part and large looped curls at each side. Costume: rose satin gown with lace and floral trim, taffeta frou-frou petticoat, pantalets, velvet shoes, with bouquet of flowers and "diamond" earrings. The costume is tagged Jenny Lind and the doll has her original wrist booklet and is presented in her original box labeled Jenny Lind, 1491. Excellent condition with fresh costume and complexion. Alexander, the Jenny Lind theme was so favored by Madame Alexander that she presented the doll in three different models, circa 1969. $200/400

153. "Jenny Lind" from the Portrete Series in Original Window Box, 1969

10" (25 cm.) All hard plastic with swivel head, adult-shaped torso, jointing at shoulders, hips and knees, sleep eyes, blonde hair in unusual cross-looped fashion with rosebud decorations. Costume: rose satin gown with wide panniers, lace collar, pink taffeta frou-frou petticoat, pantalets, pink sling heels, carrying bouquet of roses. The costume is labeled Jenny Lind, and the doll has an original wrist booklet and is presented in her original gold and maroon window box. Near mint condition. Alexander, 1969, model 1171. $400/600

150. "Godey" Portrait in Pink Satin and Black Velvet, 1971

21" (53 cm.) Vinyl socket head, adult modeled body, sleep eyes, blonde hair with arranged curls at the nape. Costume: pink satin gown with vertical bands of embroidered silk flowers, black velvet short jacket with beading, pink taffeta frou-frou petticoat,

154. "Bride" in Wedding Gown from Portrait Series, 1965

21" (53 cm.) Vinyl socket head, adult-lady torso, jointing at shoulders, hips and knees, high-heel posed feet, sleep eyes, blonde hair in original coiffure with nape chignon. Costume: white lace wedding gown with row of scalloped lace edging at the hem, sequin detailing at bodice and waist, tulle hem ruffle, large white satin flounces at the back, tulle veil with coronet of large white flowers that matches her bridal bouquet, taffeta petticoat and long pantalets, stockings, white sling heels, pearl necklace and dangle earrings, solitaire ring. Her costume is labeled Alexander and she has her original wrist booklet and original box. Near mint condition. Alexander, 1965, model 2151, the doll was featured on the catalog cover for that year. $500/700

155. "Queen" from Portrait Series, 1965

21" (53 cm.) Vinyl socket head, adult-lady shaped torso, jointing at shoulders, hips and knees, high-heel posed feet, sleep eyes, wheat blonde hair with crown chignon and shoulder length curls. Costume: gold brocade gown with fitted bodice, blue taffeta banner with faux-jewels, taffeta and stiffened net petticoat, panties, stockings, gold sling heels, silver crown, pearls, faux-diamond earrings, bracelets, ring, and elbow-length gloves. The costume is labeled Alexander, and the doll has her original wrist booklet and box. Excellent condition. Alexander, 1965, model 2150, the doll appeared on the cover of the Alexander catalog that year. $300/500

156. "Southern Belle" Portrait Model, 1965

21" (53 cm.) Vinyl socket head, adult-lady shaped torso, jointing at shoulders, hips and knees, high-heel posed feet, sleep eyes, golden blonde hair in very elaborate coiffure with a series of arranged curls, tiny braids, and ringlets interwoven with rhinestone hair ornaments. Costume: sheer turquoise lavishly gathered gown with beaded lace bodice, and pleated ruffled at neck, cuffs and hem, decorated with sprigs of sweetheart roses, pale aqua taffeta petticoat, panties, stockings, silver sling heels, diamond earrings, solitaire and double-band blue "sapphire" bracelet. The costume is tagged Alexander, the doll has original wrist booklet, and original box. Near mint condition, gorgeous coiffure that is perfectly preserved, beautiful facial complexion, very fresh and vibrant costume, minor green on wrist under bracelet. Alexander, 1965, the doll was presented on the cover of their 1965 catalog named "Southern Belle". $500/800

157. "Melanie" from Portrait Series, 1967

21" (53 cm.) Vinyl socket head, adult-lady shaped torso, jointed shoulders, hips and knees, high-heel posed feet, sleep eyes, blonde hair in original elaborate coiffure. Costume: turquoise taffeta gown with braid trim, frou-frou petticoat, panties, stockings, turquoise satin shoes, white woven bonnet with generous cluster of white flowers and violets at the crown, and turquoise tulle streamers, solitaire. The costume is labeled Melanie, and the doll has her original wrist booklet, and box. Near mint condition. Alexander, the doll appeared in the 1967 catalog, model 2173. $300/600

158. "Melinda" from Portrette Series, 1968

10" (25 cm.) All hard plastic with socket head, adult-lady shaped torso, jointing at shoulders, hips and knees, high-heel posed feet. Costume: nearly identical to #157, Melanie, with variations in trim, flowers, and shoes. The costume is labeled Melinda, and the doll has her original wrist tag and original labeled gold and maroon window box. Near mint condition. Alexander, 1968, model 1173, from the "portrette" series "inspired by the many requests for 11" reproductions of important annual collections of Portrait Dolls" according to the 1968 Alexander catalog that introduced the dolls. $300/500

159. "Renoir" from Portrait Series, 1967

21" (53 cm.) Vinyl socket head, adult-lady shaped torso, jointing at hips, shoulders and knees, high-heel posed feet, brown sleep eyes, brunette hair with arranged curly bangs and curls at nape. Costume: navy blue taffeta gown with pleated skirt ruffles, fitted jacket with ruffled lapels and lace trimmed cuffs, taffeta frou-frou petticoat, panties, red taffeta bonnet with red flowers, red satin heeled shoes, flowers at waist, pearl earrings and solitaire. The costume is labeled Renoir, the doll has original wrist booklet and original box. Near mint condition. Alexander, 1967, model 2175, the doll was the only portrait model to appear on the cover of the 1967 catalog. $300/500

160. "Renoir" from Portrette Series, 1968

10" (25 cm.) All hard plastic doll with socket head, adult-shaped torso, jointing at shoulders, hips and knees, high-heel posed feet, brunette wig. Costume: navy blue taffeta gown that is a near duplicate to her matching 21" sister, except this gown is one piece (without separate jacket). The costume is labeled Renoir, and the doll has original wrist booklet and original gold and maroon window box. Near mint condition. Alexander, model 1175 from the 1968 Portrette series, created, according to the Alexander catalog, to meet the demands of miniature models of the 21" portrait dolls. $400/600

162. Maggie "Dressed in the Fashion of Her Day", 1972

17" (43 cm.) Vinyl socket head, jointing at shoulders and hips, large green sleep eyes, long straight reddish/brown hair with bangs. Costume: pleated plaid skirt with attached white cotton bodice, under green felt double-breasted jacket, slip, panties, stockings, black velvet flat shoes, woven straw boater with green band and bow. The costume is labeled "Maggie" and the doll has her original Maggie booklet and original box. Near mint condition. Alexander, model 1720, 1972, described in that year's catalog as "dressed in the fashion of her day." $200/400

163. Wendy-Kins "McGuffey Ana", 1965

8" (20 cm.) All hard plastic, socket head, jointing at shoulders and hips, bent knees, sleep eyes, blonde hair with curly bangs and braids. Costume: red and white checkered school dress under white cut-work pinafore, petticoat, pantalets, socks, black shoes, white woven bonnet with red band and flowers. The costume is labeled McGuffey Ana and she has her original "Friends from Storyland" wrist tag and original box. Near mint condition. Alexander, 1965, model 388. $200/300

161. "Sweetie Walker", 1962

23" (58 cm.) All rigid vinyl, socket head of plump-faced little girl, jointing at shoulders and hips, blonde bobbed hair with rolled curl at the crown tied with rose silk ribbon. Costume: pink dotted Swiss dress and rompers under a pink polished pique short coat, socks, shoes. The costume is labeled Alexander, and the doll has original wrist booklet "Sweetie Walker" and is in original box. Near mint condition. Alexander, model 7920, 1962, the doll was described in the Alexander catalog of that year as "supreme artistry of doll making...with face of great appeal." $200/250

164. Complete Seven Doll Set of "Sound of Music", 1971

The set includes three 8" dolls, Friedrich, Marta, and Gretl; three 10" dolls, Loyise, Liesl, and Brigitte, and 12" Maria, each with original coiffure to represent their character in the Sound of Music film that was released in 1965. Costumes: each is wearing its original Tyrolean style costume. Each doll has its original costume label, wrist booklet, and is presented in its original box. Near mint condition. Alexander, 1971, the dolls appeared in that year's catalog as a re-creation of the Trapp Family featured in the Sound of Music film. $1000/1500

165. Wendy-Kins "Colonial Girl", 1962-1964

8" (20 cm.) All hard plastic, socket head, jointing at shoulders and hips, bendable knee walking style body, sleep eyes, blonde hair drawn away from face and captured into curls at the nape. Costume: blue chambray dress with large white collar, white apron, white cap, petticoat, panties, socks, black shoes, carrying basket of fruit. The costume is labeled "Colonial Girl" and the doll has original Colonial Girl booklet and is in original labeled box. Near mint condition. Alexander, model 789, the doll was made from 1962-1964. $200/300

166. Wendy-Kins "Mary, Mary", from Storyland Dolls Series, 1965-1972

8" (20 cm.) All hard plastic with socket head, jointing at shoulders and hips, bendable knees, sleep eyes, blonde hair captured in curls at crown, and falling onto her shoulders. Costume: cotton flowered dress under pink cotton apron with deep pockets that hold flowers, lace-edged petticoat and pantalets, socks, black shoes, carrying blue plastic watering can. The costume is labeled Mary, Mary, the doll has original "Little Women" wrist booklet, and is in her original box. Near mint condition. Alexander, model 0751, the doll was made from 1966-1972. $200/300

167. "Madame Pompadour" Portrait Doll, 1970

21" (53 cm.) Vinyl socket head, adult-lady shaped torso, jointing at shoulders, hips and knees, sleep eyes, very long curled lashes, blonde hair in very ornate style of late 18th century. Costume: pink satin and brocade gown with wide panniers, lace edging, feathered hair ornaments, frou-frou petticoat, pantalets, stockings, pink sling heels, fan, faux-diamond earrings, solitaire and necklace. The costume is labeled Alexander, and the doll has her original wrist booklet and original box. Near mint condition. Alexander, model 2197, 1970. $400/500

168. "Mimi" from Portrait Series, 1971

21" (53 cm.) Vinyl socket head, adult-lady shaped torso, jointing at shoulders, hips and knees, high-heel posed feet, sleep eyes, blonde hair in elaborate arrangement of ringlet curls. Costume: white taffeta gown with pink soutache trim under a brilliant pink taffeta full-length evening coat with pink tulle wrap that matching the pink tulle-swatched hat, pale pink rose decorations, frou-frou petticoat, pantalets, silver sling heels. The costume is labeled "Mimi", the doll has original wrist booklet and original labeled box. Near mint condition. Alexander, the portrait "Mimi" appeared for one year only, model 2170, 1970. $300/500

169. "Godey" Portrait, 1970

21" (53 cm.) Vinyl socket head, adult-lady shaped torso, jointing at shoulders, hips and knees, high-heel posed feet, sleep eyes, brunette hair in ornate coiffure. Costume: shadow-stripe pink satin gown with lace ruffles at the bodice, purple velvet short jacket with "jewel" clasp closure, frou-frou pink taffeta petticoat, pantalets, stockings, pink sling shoes, lavender tulle flounce bonnet with long tulle streamers and floral decorations, pearl earrings. solitaire. The costume is labeled Alexander, the doll has original wrist booklet, and is in original box. Near mint condition. Alexander, Godey, model 2195 from the 1970 series. $200/400

170. "Lady Hamilton" Portrait Doll, 1968

21" (53 cm.) Vinyl socket head, adult-lady shaped torso, jointing at shoulders, hips and knees, high-heel posed feet, sleep eyes, blonde hair with bangs and ringlet curls. Costume: gown of ecru lace over pink taffeta with pouf sleeves, rose satin sash, flowers, pink taffeta frou-frou petticoat, panties, stockings, rose velvet shoes, woven wide-brimmed bonnet with rose satin and floral trim, pearl necklace and bracelet, dangle pearl earrings. The costume is labeled Alexander, the doll has original wrist booklet and is in her original labeled box. Near mint condition. Alexander, model 2182, from the 1968 portrait series. $300/500

171. "Renoir" from Premiere Year of Portrait Series, 1965

21" (53 cm.) Vinyl socket head, adult-shaped lady torso, jointing at hips, shoulders and knees, high-heel posed feet, brown sleep eyes, red hair in center-part with ringlet curls. Costume: pink taffeta sleeveless gown with arched circlets of narrow ruffled pleats and lace trim, matching fitted short jacket with passamenterie edging, matching poke bonnet, white tulle petticoat, panties, stockings, silver sling heels, diamond earrings, bracelet and solitaire ring. The costume is labeled Alexander, and the doll has her original wrist booklet and box. Near mint condition. Alexander, model 2154, 1965, the initial year of the Jacqueline-face portrait series. $400/700

172. "Goya" Portrait Doll, 1968

21" (53 cm.) Vinyl socket head, adult-lady shaped torso, jointing at shoulders, hips and knees, high-heel posed feet, blonde hair in ornate fashion, sleep eyes with very long lashes. Costume: pink taffeta gown with eight tiers of skirt ruffles, lacy tiered pouf sleeves, pink taffeta "beehive" bonnet with floral trim and pink streamers, pink taffeta frou-frou petticoat, panties, stockings, coral satin heels, solitaire. The costume is labeled Alexander, and the doll has her original wrist booklet and original box. Near mint condition. Alexander, model 2183, 1968. $400/600

173. "Godey" Portrait in Red Velvet, 1969

21" (53 cm.) Vinyl socket head, adult-lady shaped torso, jointing at shoulders, hips and knees, high-heel posed feet, sleep eyes, long curly lashes, blonde hair. Costume: red velvet strapless gown with flared skirt under fitted jacket that extends nearly to the floor and is edged with black braid trim and jet buttons, taffeta frou-frou petticoat, pantalets, stockings, red sling heels, black woven bonnet with red satin bows and dramatic netting, black lace fingerless gloves, faux-ruby-and-diamond earrings and matching necklace. The costume is labeled Alexander, the doll has original wrist booklet and original box labeled Godey 2195. Near mint condition. Alexander, model 2195, the doll is shown on the cover of the 1969 Alexander catalog. $300/500

174. "Scarlett" Portrait in Red Velvet Gown with Brooch and Watch, 1960s

21" (53 cm.) Vinyl socket head, adult-lady shaped torso, jointing at shoulders, hips and knees, high-heel posed feet, sleep eyes, dark brunette hair with classic 1860s style ringlet curls. Costume: red velvet sleeveless gown with generous lace jabot, matching red velvet fitted jacket with lace edging, two stiffened tulle petticoats, panties, stockings, red sling heels, red velvet bonnet with modesty brim and white flowers, gold-plated brooch with attached "diamond" framed watch, solitaire. The costume is labeled Alexander, the doll has original wrist booklet, and the doll is presented in her original box labeled Scarlett with curious model number "6503". Near mint condition, beautiful complexion. Alexander, 1960s, year uncertain, the model number on the original box is unusual. $400/600

175. "Coco" as "Scarlett", 1966

21" (53 cm.) Vinyl socket head with unique sculpting for this model, adult-lady shaped torso with unique swivel waist, jointing at shoulders and hips, legs posed in classic model manner with sculpted bent right knee, brown sleep eyes, brunette hair with very full bangs and long flowing curls. Costume: lace and sheer tulle white gown with fitted bodice, red satin sash, sweetheart roses appliques, taffeta petticoat, panties, stockings, tan slipper shoes with red bows, white woven wide-brimmed bonnet with white flowers at the brim, solitaire. The costume is labeled Alexander and the doll has her original wrist booklet and box labeled Scarlett 2061 with original store price label of $30. Near mint condition, gorgeous complexion and beautifully fresh and vibrant costume. Alexander, from the Coco series of 1966. $800/1200

176. "Scarlett" Portrait in Flowered Gown, 1968
21" (53 cm.) Vinyl socket head, adult-lady shaped torso, jointing at shoulders, hips and knees, high-heel posed feet, green sleep eyes, long curly lashes, long flowing brunette curls. Costume: flowered cream cotton gown with wide white pleated border, green velvet sash that matches the green velvet band on wide-brimmed woven bonnet, stiffened tulle petticoat, panties, stockings, green heels, silk taffeta parasol, cameo necklace and solitaire. The costume is labeled Scarlett, the doll has her original wrist booklet and original box labeled Scarlett 2180. Near mint condition. Alexander, model 2180, the doll was featured on the cover of the Alexander 1968 catalog. $400/600

177. Wendy-kins "Scarlett" with White Cotton Gown, Circa 1968
8" (20 cm.) All hard plastic with swivel head, jointing at shoulder and hips, bendable knees, brunette hair with flip curls, green sleep eyes. Costume: white cotton gown printed with delicate pink and blue flowers and trimmed with green rick-rack, green satin sash, stiffened petticoat, pantalets with green silk ribbon trim, socks, black flat shoes, wide woven bonnet with green streamers. The costume is labeled Scarlett and she has her original wrist booklet and box. Near mint condition. Alexander, model 725, circa 1968. $200/400

178. Wendy-Kins "Scarlett" with Cream Flowered Gown, Circa 1968
8" (20 cm.) All hard plastic with swivel head, jointed shoulder and hips, bendable knees, green sleep eyes, brunette hair with flip curls. Costume: cream cotton flowered gown printed with delicate rose buds and trimmed with green rick-rack,

green satin sash and bonnet streamers, wide-brimmed woven bonnet, stiffened petticoat, pantalets with green ribbons, socks, black flat shoes. The costume is labeled Scarlett and the doll has her original wrist booklet and original box labeled Scarlett 725. Near mint condition. Alexander, model 725, circa 1968. $200/400

179. "Gone With The Wind", Dolls from the Classics Series, 1968

14" (36 cm.) Vinyl socket head, five piece body with jointing at shoulders and hips, green sleep eyes, brunette shoulder length curly wig. Costume: the doll is wearing cream cotton gown printed with delicate wildflowers and leaves, with green ribbon and lace trimmed bodice, green velvet sash to match the streamers of her wide-brimmed bonnet, stiffened petticoat, pantalets with cut-work ruffles, stockings, flat black shoes. The costume is labeled Scarlett, and the doll has her original box labeled Gone with the Wind, 1495. Near mint condition. Alexander, model 1495, from the Dolls from the Classics series of 1968. $200/400

180. "Scarlett" Portrait in Green Taffeta, 1970

21" (53 cm.) Vinyl socket head, adult-lady shaped torso, jointing at shoulders, hips and knees, green sleep eyes, brunette flowing curls. Costume: green taffeta gown with matching green taffeta fitted jacket, each trimmed with white braid, matching bonnet with white roses, frou-frou petticoat, pantalets with green ribbon and lace, stockings, green sling heels. The costume is labeled Scarlett, and the doll has her original wrist booklet and box labeled Scarlett 2190. Near mint condition. Alexander, although the box is labeled 2190, it appears to mis-stamped as the doll is identical to model 2180 from the 1970 catalog. $400/600

181. Cissette "Southern Belle" from Portrette Series, 1971

10" (25 cm.) All hard plastic, socket head, adult-lady shaped torso, jointing at shoulders, hips and knees, high-heel posed feet, brown sleep eyes, brunette hair. Costume: white organdy gown with four rows of lace on the skirt, red satin sash, frou-frou petticoat, lace-edged pantalets, stockings, white sling heels, white woven hat with blue and red flowers and white tulle flounce. heart locket. The costume is labeled Southern Belle, and the doll has her original paper booklet and labeled box. Near mint condition. Alexander, model 1185, 1971. $300/500

182. Cissette "Southern Belle" from the Portrette Series, 1973

10" (25 cm.) All hard plastic, socket head, adult-lady shaped torso, jointing at hips, shoulders and knees, high-heel posed feet, brown sleep eyes, brunette hair. Costume: white organdy gown with four rows of lace and green satin sash, stiffened tulle frou-frou petticoat, pantalets, stockings, white sling heels, wide-brimmed white bonnet trimmed with delicate white flowers and tulle, gold heart locket. The costume is tagged "Southern Belle" and the doll has original wrist booklet and original box labeled Southern Belle 1184. Near mint condition. Alexander, model 1184, 1973. $300/500

183. Cissette "Melinda" from Portrette Series, 1969

10" (25 cm.) All hard plastic, socket head, adult-lady shaped torso, jointing at shoulders, hips and knees, blonde hair in soft curls with pink bows and tiny flowers. Costume: pink organdy gown with ten tiers of pink ruffled lace, pink sash with tiny rosebuds at the center waist. pink taffeta frou-frou petticoat, panties, stockings, pink sling heels. The costume is labeled Melinda and the doll has her original wrist booklet and original gold and maroon window box. Near mint condition. Alexander, model 1173, 1969. $300/500

184. Cissette "Scarlett" from Portrette Series, 1970

10" (25 cm.) All hard plastic, socket head, adult-lady shaped torso, jointing at shoulders and hips, bendable knees, high-heel posed feet, green sleep eyes, brunette long curly hair. Costume: green taffeta gown and matching jacket with black braid trim, matching bonnet with pink flower, frou-frou petticoat, pantalets with lace edging, black sling heels, black cameo necklace. The costume is labeled Scarlett and the doll has her original box labeled Scarlett 1181. Near mint condition. Alexander, model 1181, 1970. $300/500

185. Cissette "Agathe" from Portrette Series, 1969

10" (25 cm.) All hard plastic, socket head, adult-lady modeled torso, jointing at shoulders and hips, bendable knees, high-heel posed feet, sleep eyes, brunette hair. Costume: red velvet gown with ecru lace at the neckline and cuffs, matching red bonnet with braid edging and tulle trim, frou-frou petticoat, panties, stockings, black heeled shoes, faux-diamond brooch. The costume is labeled Agatha and the doll has original wrist tag and original gold and maroon window box. Excellent condition. Alexander, model 1171, 1968. $300/500

186. Cissette "Renoir" from Portrette Series, 1970

10" (25 cm.) All hard plastic, socket head, adult-lady shaped torso, jointing at shoulders and hips, bendable knees, high-heel posed feet, sleep eyes, brunette hair with unusual short curls framing her face and long captured curls at her nape. Costume: pale blue taffeta gown with narrow pleats at the hem, lace collar with large centered flower, frou-frou petticoat, panties, blue sling heels, pale blue woven hat with four large shaded flowers and tulle. The costume is labeled Renoir and the doll has her original box labeled Renoir 1180. Near mint condition. Alexander, model 1180, 1970. $300/500

187. Cissette "Godey" from Portrette Series, 1968

10" (25 cm.) All hard plastic, socket head, adult-lady shaped body, jointing at shoulders and hips, bendable knees, high-heel posed feet, sleep eyes, auburn hair in

elaborate coiffure. Costume: pink taffeta fitted gown with lace overlay on torso and sleeves, ruffles at skirt, pink taffeta bows extending down the bodice, pink taffeta frou-frou petticoat, panties, stockings, pink satin heels, woven bonnet decorated with dainty flowers, leaves and tulle flounce. The costume is labeled Godey and the doll has her original wrist tag and gold and maroon window box. Near mint condition. Alexander, model 1172, 1968 $300/500

188. Cissette "Godey" from Portrette Series, 1969

10" (25 cm.) All hard plastic, socket head, adult-lady shaped body, jointing at shoulders and hips, bendable knees, high-heel posed feet, sleep eyes, auburn hair in elaborate coiffure. Costume: matching costume to #187 except of yellow taffeta, with variation of woven bonnet having upturned brim and decoration with white tulle and flowers. The costume is labeled Godey and the doll is in her original box labeled Godey 1172. Near mint condition. Alexander, model 1172, 1969. $300/500

189. "Melanie" Portrait, 1968

21" (53 cm.) Vinyl socket head, adult-lady shaped torso, jointing at shoulders and hips, bendable knees, high-heel posed feet, brown sleep eyes, brunette hair in center-part captured with snood at the nape. Costume: rust-brown faille strapless gown with matching short fitted jacket, each trimmed with elaborate braid and lace, frou-frou petticoat, panties, stockings, brown heeled shoes, brown velvet lace-edged bonnet and matching tasseled bag, "diamond"-edged black cameo, solitaire. The costume is labeled Melanie and the doll is presented in original box labeled Melanie 2181. Excellent condition. Alexander, model 2181, the doll was shown on the cover of the 1968 Alexander catalog. $500/700

190. "Melanie" Portrait, 1970

21" (53 cm.) Vinyl socket head, adult-shaped lady body, jointing at shoulders and hips, bendable knees, high-heel posed feet, brown sleep eyes, brunette hair in side-captured ringlet curls. Costume: white nylon dotted Swiss gown trimmed with lace and red satin ribbons, frou-frou petticoat, pantalets with red silk ribbons, red sling heels, white woven wide-brimmed bonnet with red roses and white tulle flounces, red satin parasol, "diamond"-edged cameo necklace. The costume is labeled Melanie. Excellent condition. Alexander, model 2196, 1970. $300/500

191. "Renoir" Portrait Doll, 1969

21" (53 cm.) Vinyl socket head, adult-lady shaped torso, jointing at shoulders and hips, bendable knees, high-heel posed feet, brown sleep eyes, brunette hair in elaborate coiffure. Costume: yellow taffeta fitted gown with lace overlay, yellow taffeta sash with wide taffeta flounces at the back, yellow taffeta frou-frou petticoat, pantalets, gold sling heels, yellow woven bonnet with upturned brim decorated with dainty violets and yellow tulle, pearl drop earrings, "diamond"-edged black cameo. The costume is tagged Renoir and the doll has her original wrist booklet and box labeled Renoir 2194. Near mint condition. Alexander, model 2194, the doll was photographed on the cover of the Alexander 1969 catalog. $400/600

192. "Renoir" Portrait, 1973

21" (53 cm.) Vinyl socket head, adult-lady shaped torso, jointing at shoulders and hips, bendable knees, high-heel posed feet, brown sleep eyes, blonde hair in elaborate curls. Costume: golden yellow taffeta gown with ruffles at skirt hem, frou-frou petticoat, pantalets, yellow sling heels, woven hat with clusters of flowers and tulle flounce, solitaire. The costume is labeled Renoir and the doll has her original wrist booklet and box labeled Renoir 2190. Near mint condition. Alexander, model 2190, 1973. $300/400

193. Elise Queen for FAO Schwarz, 1973

17" (43 cm.) Vinyl socket head, five piece body, sleep eyes, ash blonde hair in elaborate coiffure. Costume: gold brocade gown with blue and red taffeta banner with faux-jewels, petticoat, panties, stockings, ecru satin shoes, jewelry including pearls, earrings, ring, and three bracelets, and elaborate "diamond" crown. The costume is labeled Elise, and the doll has original wrist booklet and box labeled Elise 1790. Near mint condition. Alexander, model 1790, 1973, the box has store label from FAO Schwarz and may have been an exclusive for that luxury toy store. $200/400

194. Cissette "Queen", 1972

10" (25 cm.) All hard plastic, socket head, adult-lady shaped torso, jointing at shoulders and hips, bendable knees, high-heel posed feet, sleep eyes, ash blonde hair. Costume: white satin brocade gown with red taffeta banner decorated with "faux" jewels, petticoat, panties, stockings, white sling heels, pearl necklace, and crown with faux-jewel ruby and diamonds. The costume is labeled Queen and the doll has original booklet and original box labeled Queen 1186. Near mint condition. Alexander, model 1186, 1972/73, the doll was presented on the 20th anniversary of Queen Elizabeth's coronation. $300/400

195. Wendy-Kins "Miss U.S.A." from Americana Series, 1966

8" (20 cm.) All hard plastic, socket head, jointing at shoulders and hips, bendable knees, sleep eyes, golden blonde hair. Costume: white nylon organza gown with red and blue flowing scarf fastened with brass-framed "diamond", petticoat, panties, gold

shoes, ornate brass crown with seven "diamonds". The costume is labeled U.S.A. and the doll has her original booklet and box labeled U.S.A. 728. Near mint condition. Alexander, model 728, from the Americana Series of 1966. $200/400

196. Brenda Starr "Wearing Chic Shirt-Waist Dress", 1964

12" (30 cm.) Vinyl socket head, slender hard plastic body with adult-lady shape, jointing at shoulders, hips and knees, high-heel posed feet, sleep eyes, auburn hair in bouffant style with arranged topknot. Costume: pink cotton shirtwaist dress with white lace lower skirt, cotton petticoat and matching satin panties, white plastic heels and purse, pearl earrings. The costume is labeled Brenda Starr, and the doll has original booklet describing "the many ways you can arrange her lovely golden hair", and box labeled Brenda Starr 915. Near mint condition. Alexander, model 915, 1964, and has original store tag from I.Magnin. $300/500

197. Brenda Starr "Wearing a Stunning Outfit", 1964

12" (30 cm.) Vinyl socket head, slender hard plastic body with adult-lady shape, jointing at shoulders, hips and knees, sleep eyes, auburn bouffant coiffure with topknot. Costume: blue nylon knit sheath with attached swirling cape that attaches at the collar with two tiny rosebuds, panties, black heels, pearl earrings. The costume is labeled Brenda Starr and the doll has original booklet and box labeled Brenda

Starr 921. Near mint condition. Alexander model 921, the doll appeared on the cover of the Alexander catalog in 1964. $300/500

198. "Polly" Ballerina, 1965

17" (43 cm.) Vinyl socket head, five piece body, sleep eyes, dark brunette waist-length hair with bangs. Costume: turquoise tulle tutu with sequined bodice, satin turquoise attached panties with tulle ruffle, ecru satin shoes with ankle ties, rose velvet throat ribbon, coronet of rose and white flowers and leaves, solitaire. The costume is labeled "Polly", the doll has original wrist booklet, and is presented in original box labeled Polly 1725. Near mint condition. Alexander, model 1725, the doll was made for one year only in 1965 described as "our new glamorous young lady" advertised as having pink tulle tutu; this example made be an special production doll. $300/500

199. Elise in Pink Gown with Ruffled Bodice, FAO Schwarz Special, 1966

17" (43 cm.) Uniquely-shaded reddish-brown hair in elaborate side-swept coiffure with arranged curls at the back crown and sides of face, decorated with tiny flowers. Costume: sheer pink nylon gown with narrowly pleated full skirt, five tiers of lace ruffles on the bodice with metallic silver braid trim, pink taffeta petticoat, panties, stockings, silver heeled shoes, bouquet of flowers. Near mint condition. The costume is labeled Elise. Alexander, the doll was a store exclusive for FAO Schwarx in 1966. $300/500

200. Elise Bride, 1972

17" (43 cm.) Having long straight red hair captured at nape, sleep eyes. Costume: white tulle wedding gown with bead-crusted lace bodice, full length veil with lavish lace trim and floral coronet that matches her bouquet, petticoat, panties, ecru satin shoes, pearl earrings. The costume is labeled Madame Alexander and she has her original wrist booklet and original hard-sided box labeled Elsie 1760. Near mint condition. Alexander, model 1760, 1972. $200/300

201. Elise in Pink Ball Gown, 1973

17" (43 cm.) Ash blonde hair in very elaborate arranged curls at crown and nape. Costume: two layers of delicate pink tulle, the outer layer with bands of pink lace that matches the lace bodice and pouf sleeves, pink taffeta petticoat, panties, stockings, pink satin heeled shoes, pink satin sash, shaded pink flowers in hair, pearl necklace and earrings. solitaire. The costume is labeled Madame Alexander, the doll has original wrist tag, and is in her original hard-sided box labeled Elise 1755. Near mint condition. Alexander, model 1755, 1973, with original store label of FAO Schwarz on the box. $200/400

202. "Elise Portrait" in Pink Gown with Bonnet, 1972

17" (43 cm.) With long flowing platinum blonde hair. Costume: pink sheer nylon gown with ruffles at bodice, pleated wide band at skirt decorated with rosebuds, pink taffeta sash, taffeta petticoat, panties, ecru satin shoes, pink woven wide-brimmed bonnet with lavish multi-colored flowers, "diamond" brooch and solitaire. The costume is labeled Madame Alexander, she has original wrist booklet and original hard-sided box labeled Portrait 1780. Near mint condition. Alexander, model 1780, the doll was named "Portrait Elise" in the 1972 catalog. $200/300

203. Elise Ballerina in Yellow Tutu, 1973

17" (43 cm.) Ash blonde hair captured in long loose chignon at nape of neck. Costume: wearing yellow tulle and satin tutu with cascading cluster of flowers at her waist, yellow ballet slippers, black velvet neck ribbon, pearl drop earrings, coronet of flowers. The costume is labeled Madame Alexander and she has original wrist tag and original hard-sided box labeled Elise 1745. Near mint condition. Alexander, model 1745, 1973. $200/300